SOUL-FULLNESS

Books, Audio & Video materials by Tosin King James:
Available at all online and retail stores worldwide.
www.tosinkingjames.com
@tosinkingjames

SOUL-FULLNESS

Tosin King James

Soul-Fullness

Copyright © 2021 Tosin James

All rights reserved. No part of this book may be reproduced, stored in a retrieval system, or transmitted in any form by any means, whether electronic, mechanical, photocopying, recording, or otherwise, without prior written permission of the author, except in the case of brief quotations embodied in critical articles and review.

ISBN: 978-1-7377260-0-5

Cover concept and design:
Shashika (fiver.com/shashika2), and Tosin King James
Page design: Didier Rogers
Illustrations: Taiwo Deji (fiver.com/grafiksmill), and Zeera
Editing: Ira McIntyre & 'Tayo Keyede (reedsy.com/keyede-tayo)
Models & photography: istockphotos.com, pixabay.com
Extra photography and modeling: Zeera

Thematic contributions:
Vivian James
Amechi Chukwujama
Motunde Adewunmi
Afo Kanu

An imprint of Zeera LLC
21213 Hawthorne Blvd, Torrance, CA 90503, USA
www.zeeramedia.com

DEDICATION

To all true seekers
who have genuinely surrendered,
and have found;
and the benevolent Lords and Saints,
Guardians to a spiritually asleep race.

CONTENTS

Foreword: Secrets of Soul-Fullness ... ix

Soul-Fullness ... 1

Day One: A Moment in the Future ... 3

Day Two: Open Your Eyes ... 11

Day Three: Open Your Ears ... 15

Day Four: Clean Up the Physical Temple ... 23

Day Five: Clean Up the Emotional Temple ... 29

Day Six: Clean Up the Mental Temple ... 39

Day Seven: Develop Language of Communication with Spirit ... 47

Day Eight: Gratitude I: Thank God for Life ... 53

Day Nine: Gratitude II: Thank God for Your Material Possessions ... 57

Day Ten: Gratitude III: Thank God for Wisdom ... 63

Day Eleven: Gratitude IV: Be Grateful for the Love in Your Life ... 71

Day Twelve: Gratitude V: Love Your Body and Thank God for It ... 77

Day Thirteen: Gratitude VI: Thank God for Your Enemies — 83

Day Fourteen: Gratitude VII: Thank God for the Good in the Life of Others — 87

Day Fifteen: Invite and Meet Your Guardian Angel — 93

Day Sixteen: Converse with Your Guardian Angel — 101

Day Seventeen: Land of the Orange Sun — 109

Day Eighteen: Visit Tomorrow — 116

Day Nineteen: Another Visit to Tomorrow — 123

Day Twenty: Place Yourself in Your Future — 129

Day Twenty-One: Faith and Gratitude — 137

Soul-Fullness: Principles — 141

After the Book: Spiritual Encounters — 151

After the Book II: Conversation in Paradise on Death and the Aftermath — 175

Preface to *The Book of Prophecies* — 185

About the Author — 199

Glossary — 201

FOREWORD

SECRETS OF SOUL-FULLNESS AND HOW TO DO IT YOURSELF

Soul-Fullness is the conscious and practical application of Soul's innate abilities, skills, and resources to achieve enhanced wisdom, love, creativity, and freedom. In its short form, it is simply operating from, and with, the fullness of Soul.

This 21-day program was designed with the help of the Spirit Guardians in May 2014. The template was published as *See Your Future in 21 Days*. In its present form as *Soul-Fullness*, the original template is intact but has been beefed up with additional techniques and feedbacks from those who practiced the program. Miracles of elevation in consciousness, physical healing, emotional healing, visions, and prophecies were experienced worldwide. There were also those who began to dream consciously; those who traveled to the Heavens; those who experienced the presence of the Spirit Guardians; and those who received protection from physical and psychic harm. The 'mundane' miracles also came in the form of better jobs, career advancement, finding a more loving relationship, and even buying that dream house and car.

There Is No 'You'; There Is Only 'I Am'

There is no limit to what we can achieve when we tap consciously into the fullness of Soul. Let me make some clarifications about Soul and spiritual potentialities. Soul is what I am. Soul is always 'I Am', never 'you', 'him', 'her', 'they', and 'we'. It is the indestructible, eternal, genderless, Unit of Life, that devolves from the Original Source of all Life. In religious terms, the Original Source of Life has been referred to as God, Holy Spirit, Higher Power, Higher Self, the Word, consciousness, etc.

Being a Unit of Life, It contains the potential of being omniscient, omnipresent, and omnipotent. However, because It is encased in the husk, box, cloak, or shell known as the body and mind, It appears to be half asleep, ignorant, powerless, fearful, hateful, selfish, and destructive. But when It is freed from the cage, like an eagle, It soars into the far reaches of the heavens. Not even the clouds can limit Its ascent.

But all these definitions and explanations mean nothing until you have experienced yourself as Soul. Paradoxically, that is the end goal of religion, metaphysics, science, yoga, sports, sex, greed, anger, patience, selfishness, and selflessness. Sounds strange? Oh, yes! It is strange until you have realized yourself as a Unit of Life, a.k.a. Spirit.

The Five Stages of Unfoldment of Soul

On that long journey, there are many portals through which everyone passes, but not at the same time. This is the beauty of spiritual unfoldment. The road map is the same, but each travels at their own pace.

Stage One: Here, we think we are the body. So, we nurture, adore, and idolize it. Then, when the body whittles, loses its vibrancy and starts accelerating towards a complete breakdown and dissolution, we become frustrated, confused, and cannot understand what this life is all about.

Stage Two: We become aware of our emotions, how powerful and persuasive they can be if we choose our attachments and identifications tactically. We begin to identify with groups — family, nationality, club, religion — for the sake of relevance and protection.

Stage Three: We become aware of the power of imagination. If we can dream it, we can make it happen. We begin to seek teachers, paths, techniques, and science to dominate our environment, property, people's approval, and power. Here, we seek gods that can make things happen. The gods can be metaphysical or material.

Stage Four: We discover the power of the mind and how meaning is infused into everything we see, feel, and think. This is the Cartesian portal where 'I think, therefore I am' rules our worldview. Here, our ultimate is the philosophy and leaders of thought, ideologies, concepts, symbolism, and religions that are based on the power of positive thinking.

Stage Five: The fifth portal is that of Soul-Fullness. Here, we realize that we are not the body, not the emotions, not the mind. We realize we are the 'I Am' that brings all into being. Our body, mind, and emotions are ours, but they are tools, just like the tractor is to the farmer, and the car is to the driver. We love these tools, but we know we are greater, better than our tools. The body will die; the emotions are transient; the mind is limited though it is as elastic as the universe. But Soul is eternal, predating all of life and surviving the collapse, decay, and dissolution of body, mind, and imagination.

Soul-Fullness shows us how to enhance the limitless power of Soul to get things done while we are here in our beautiful cage. It also helps us apprehend and comprehend the invisible layers of life that are otherwise imperceptible to the five senses, the imagination, and the mind. Beyond meditation and mental practices, Soul-Fullness assists us to contact the Origin of Life and take advantage of the gifts that come from the Higher Power and other Souls who have evolved beyond that threshold of darkness, the prison gates of the mind. These are the Spirit Guides, Guardian Angels, Avatars, Sat-Gurus, and other beings that are more powerful and wiser than what the wisest man on Earth can fathom.

Beyond the 'Collective Unconscious'

Famous depth psychologist, Carl Jung, came close to discovering the Greater Self and the Source of Life. He stopped at the 'unconscious', which he observed exists on the personal and collective levels. He was able to apprehend the workings of Spirit at the Third and Fourth Levels, where all that you have thought, felt, and imagined are stored. It is an unconscious sea of residual and latent energy. With a little more effort (and with the help of the right teacher), you can go beyond the unconscious, through the realm of super-conscious awareness. This is where you have access to all knowledge that can exist in the perishable universe. But beyond this stage, the explorer will discover the Fifth Portal of Soul. Here, you stop thinking because the mind is useless. Concepts, ideologies, religions, metaphysics, shadow, Satan, light and darkness, meditation, symbols, and archetypes all mean nothing. You realize you are that which you have sought, the meaning, the truth, the life, the path, the way, the author of your life.

This stage gives you awareness of being awake multiplied a million times. You will know things that cannot be put into words. You will experience things that have no semblance on Earth or anywhere in the galaxy.

You will stop asking questions because you are the answer. Or, better put, I Am the answer.

Soul-Fullness is a template on which you can build your own life, system, regimen, or even religion. It is not a path or religion where you need to be loyal to anyone or worship anyone. If you apply this program to your religion, beliefs, principles, love, health, and business, life will begin to have more meaning. You will love life more because you will realize, gradually, that you are Life.

The Guardians

The program has me as the scribe who downloaded it into a physical format. However, there are thousands of highly advanced beings who are working on the project to assist you, to help you succeed. The program gives you the opportunity to ask for help. I have seen dramatic transformations in the lives of everyone who has helped the cause of the book, from the editors to the book sellers, to the readers and publishers. Some of them practiced the techniques; others did not. But out of the goodness of their hearts they contributed to the success of the project. The Great Ones touched them, blessed them, and transformed them. Some of them recognized it; others did not.

Our so-called civilization has turned man into a tin god who lives in his mind and is trained to believe he can do everything with his mind. But frustration, loneliness, drug abuse, suicide, strange illnesses that have defied the magic wand of almighty science and a devaluation of human life on a grand scale are the products of the worship of the mind, ego, and individual supremacy. Soul-Fullness helps you remember and renew your bond with the Source of Life. Not in a religious, group think, group control manner, but by yourself, wherever you are.

How It All Began

Friends have asked me what led me to abandon my boisterous lifestyle to go into 'the wilderness' and subsequently changing my life's course. Here is the story.

THE CATALYST

On February 11, 2010, I had a dinner date with two lady friends from South Africa and two government functionaries. The dinner date, which was fun and enjoyable, was hosted in a popular night club in Victoria Island, Lagos. I left the venue very late in the company of one of the South African ladies. We rode in her car to Ikeja, and then parted ways, the lady going to her hotel, while I planned to hail a taxi. There was none coming my way. This was before ridesharing apps took over the planet. In the absence of a taxi or bus, I became impatient. I was anxious to get home asap. So, I decided on hitching a ride. Soon enough, a dark blue car, with heavily tinted windows, stopped for me. My mind was consumed with the urgent need to leave that spot that I ignored the warning bells in my Inner Ear as I opened the back door.

I hopped in.

As I sat down, one of the two men at the back leaned over to pull the door shut. I heard the automatic door lock snap into place. It sounded like rapid gunfire. I cringed at the touch of the dense, dark aura in the car simultaneously oozing out of both men at the back, the driver, and the smooth-talking gang leader in the passenger seat beside the driver.

"Tonight, You Die!"

It took less than thirty seconds for them to spring into

action. They took all they could find on me. But that was not enough. Their leader had extra scores to settle with me.

"Tonight, you die! I'm going to kill you!" He was angry, repeatedly hitting me in the chest with the gun.

Looking into his eyes, I knew he meant every word. He was bent on adding me to his long list of dead victims. Interestingly, I could remember these guys. I had met with them in the dream world three times in the previous six months. Every time we met, they shot or stabbed me to death. Each time, I would wake up sweating profusely, my heart racing. I would grab the pillow and peer through the window to be certain I was still alive. It was that real. I had an inner communication with the Guardians. I was told the physical event was approaching; I was going to be killed by these gangsters. But I was not ready to die. I knew I had not fulfilled my purpose of coming into the world at this time.

"What can I do to reverse this?" I asked my Guardian.

"There's a way," he replied. He gave me a technique to transmute the imminent danger from death to life, hate to love, fear to freedom. "But you will still meet."

Saved by an Angel

So, here I was with four armed men at midnight, all alone and staring death in the face. I summoned all the calm I could muster in such a condition. Then, I chanted out loud the name of my Guardian nine times. He responded. The robbers were startled. One of them asked what strange words I was uttering. Instantly, a spiritual calm took over. Suddenly, the leader changed from being angry to treating me with respect. They let me go.

From then, I knew I was living purely on Grace. All I could do in gratitude was to rededicate myself to helping all of life in the best way I could. I left everything and submitted myself to further training in the hands of the Guardians.

The Rock and the Guardian

During my ceaseless contemplation and communication with the spiritual giants, I was asked to write some books. This book was the eighth I wrote. In its first edition, it took fourteen days to write. Every day I went to a spot in the woods, by a river. On a rock there I sat, communicating with one of the Guardians, and with an android phone to write the words and techniques he dictated.

This Guardian, a slim, tall, white-bearded man, near 70 in appearance, with the skin color of Middle-Easterners, has been seen by many of the readers of the book. He is a very wise man and always represents the Source of Life. He does not want anything for himself but to see that all who hunger for truth, protection, love, and freedom are given the opportunity to find these qualities of Heaven within themselves.

Beyond Religion

It is a thing of beauty to note that religion has nothing to do with the results you will get doing this 21-day program. If you are a religious man or woman, please be faithful to your religion. Doing these techniques will only enhance your faith; it will not change it. If you do not believe in any religion, it does not matter. There is something in you greater than religion. You are Spirit. What really does that mean? You are greater than all the creations of man, including religion. You will know the truth during the program or afterward.

Start on a Sunday

The program is better started on a Sunday. You can read the book anytime you wish. The 'Spiritual Eye Technique' in the chapter, **Soul-Fullness: Principles**, can be done every night during the program, even tonight.

When we find a good thing, we keep it close to us. If you gain anything worthwhile doing this program, please continue to practice it, if possible, every month. I do so regularly. Sometimes I need help with a burdensome issue, to accomplish a daunting project, write a screenplay, or start a business. Sometimes I need more love in my heart. Sometimes I seek inner guidance at a crossroads for help with a relationship challenge. Every time I practice it, I climb the ladder a rung higher in freedom, love, and power to be the best I wish to be.

'Alice Sees Her Future Family' and Other Stories

You will enjoy over thirty real-life stories. One of them is a rare love story that began during a conscious journey to the future. Alice, in prayer, was taken to witness her future wedding and her unborn children. There are stories of healing, of higher perception, of transformation. Yes, we all can apply the guidance distilled from the experience to live a better, happier, and grander NOW.

Special Word on Suicide

The technique, **'Letter to My Older Self'**, at the end of **Day Five** is for everyone. Do it whenever life seems overwhelming. It will link you up with the Source of Life, with love and creativity buried deep inside you. Even though it may appear simple, it is good for opening the door of transformation. Please share it.

Below Installed Capacity

Man has tried all means possible to solve his daily problems and challenges, relying solely on his mind. But the more he tries, the more he is left in a quandary, confused and depressed. The reason is simple:

Humanity is operating below 'Factory Capacity' so to speak. There are abilities, skills, senses, talents, and knowledge locked up inside us, deposited there before birth. All we need do is use the right key, open the right door, enter boundless creativity, and enjoy the added power, love, freedom, and goodness that follow such an action.

THE GAS STATION MIRACLE

The benefits of Soul-Fullness can be simple and instantaneous – like in the following experience I had in Torrance, California, in January 2021.

I was driving to Santa Monica to keep an appointment. On a regular day, it is a 30-minute ride, so I had allocated 40 minutes for the journey. When I hit the road, I noticed I had just enough gas to get there. I had a choice: to buy gas now or buy it later in the day. I decided to spend five minutes to get gas. That should still give me enough time to get to Santa Monica on time.

So, I drove into a familiar station where I was sure of the quality of gas and the pumps. I picked a spot, jumped out of the car, dashed into the manager's office, paid, and dashed back to the car. I opened the tank cover, slotted the nozzle inside, and the rest went smoothly, as it should. Until I was about to pull out the nozzle. I found that it was stuck, rather firmly, inside the tank. Any attempt to apply pressure to pull it out was going to damage the tank. A few more tugs proved this was not going to be a simple gas-buying chore. This was an experience I had never had. I also did not know of anyone who had gone through this.

I checked the time. I had exactly one minute to get out of the station; otherwise I would be late for the appointment. I did not like that. I sprinted to the manager's office, told him about my predicament. His response was shocking, to say the least.

"Many of my customers have had the same problem."

"How did you resolve it?"

He scratched the back of his head, and I knew his response was not going to be comforting.

"I couldn't. I don't know how to solve this problem."

What a thing to hear the manager of a gas station say to you when one of their nozzles is annoyingly stuck in your car's tank. I was beginning to run out of patience.

"So, how did they resolve it? What did they do? At least you must have seen them do something. The fact that they're no longer here means they did something."

"I'm sorry I didn't notice how they solved the problem. I only remember that they stayed here for a long time."

"Really? Like how long?

"Maybe about two hours," he replied as calmly and as sympathetic as an undertaker. At that moment, I noticed a white car drive into the station. Unceremoniously, the manager left me to my fate to attend to the new customer.

At this point, even if the problem were resolved at that instant, I would still need to drive well above the speed limit to get to my destination as scheduled. The only option I could think of was to call Santa Monica to tell the host that I was canceling, considering I might be spending two hours here caught in a tug of war between the nozzle and the tank.

I picked my cell phone and was about to place the call when a wave of love wafted into my conscious awareness.

"Why are you not operating from the fullness of Soul?" The voice was soft, and I recognized one of the Guardians.

My hand was on the nozzle, preparing to give it another tug. I stopped. I realized I was tense, annoyed, confused, and desperate. Emotional turbulence is an effective barrier to Soul-Fullness.

I took a deep breath, sang a sacred Word, and then relaxed. What followed was surprising and exhilarating.

"Turn around. See the man wearing the white shirt. Go to him. Tell him your problem." It was the Guardian again.

There were in all seven or eight cars in the station. I saw the man with the white shirt. He was the one the manager had left me to attend to. His car was at the extreme end of the station. So, I dashed to him.

"Good day, Sir." He turned his head to look at me while securing the nozzle in his tank. As quickly and as courteous as possible, I told him of my predicament.

"Just push it in, all the way, and pull it out."

"Just like that?" I was surprised by how simple that sounded. I had tried to pull it out several times, but I had not pushed it all the way in.

"Yeah, just like that," he responded with a tone of conviviality.

I thanked him, dashed back to my car. I obeyed his instructions, and voila! Problem solved. I jumped into the car. I was about to drive off when I had the nudge to pass the knowledge to the manager, so he could help others who might soon be in the same situation.

On the highway, I sent my gratitude to Spirit, the Guardian, and the man who came to be a channel for that help. I realized that he had driven into the station when I was having the problem, after the manager had declared his helplessness. He could have gone to another station. Spirit also was definite about the person to ask for help, among the several others who were in the station, who were aware of my situation but could not help, because they simply did not know what to do.

Blessed

Later, I asked around if any of my friends had had a similar experience. Only Amalisha had witnessed someone else battling to detach nozzle from pump.

"What did he do?"

"He was at it for a long time. I think after he got fed up, he entered his car and drove away, forcefully detaching the pump from the car."

"Ouch!" I exclaimed. That must have damaged the tank, the nozzle, or the pump, or maybe all of them."

I was glad I did not have to resort to taking such a desperate action which would have been costly. Every moment of the day, we are confronted with situations where we discover our mind, logic, and all the resources available to us cannot resolve a challenge. What do we do? Turn to the all-seeing Eye of Soul, the all-knowing Pool of Wisdom, and the all-loving Heart of Spirit. How to do it? The secrets are here.

Gift from the Source and the Guardians

Soul-Fullness is a gift from the Source of Life (a.k.a. God) and the Guardians to mankind. With it, you can — and will — enter the Greater Room, a happier life, a more peaceful existence, a life of wondrous creativity and beauty.

Treasure it. Then, share it.

- *Tosin King James*

# SOUL-FULLNESS

DAY ONE

A MOMENT IN THE FUTURE

Pick a day in the future, preferably in the next six months to one year. You can also pick an event or an occasion such as your wedding, your future husband or wife (if you have not decided on him or her), your school, your health, your job and career, your children, or baby, if you are looking for a child. It can also be a random event of a particular day in the future.

Think around it. Why do you need to see or know this future day, event, person, or object? Why do you need to move into a better, healthier, happier version of yourself? The simple answer is, it is your life, after all. And you have the right to know; you have the right to dream or move into a bigger and better room in your world.

Caution

Do not investigate or control another person's future; only, and always, yours. If several parties are involved, in the case of a marriage, romantic relationship, businesses, or a political career, do not try to know the other person's future, but yours; how your life is affected by their involvement in this joint venture. The same applies in the case of better health. It should be about you. However, in the case of a minor, for whom you are responsible, you can ask Spirit to intercede, but do not dictate to Spirit.

Think clearly about how the moment in the future affects your better understanding of the present. How can you take a better decision or develop a better attitude to align yourself with the oncoming future, better health, or greater awareness of life?

THE PRESIDENT

In my second year at Obafemi Awolowo University, I was still more or less a shy student, reticent and keeping to myself for the most part. One day all that changed when I had a prophetic dream. My Guardian Angel came and took me to a time in the future, almost two years away. In the experience, I was standing in front of thousands of students and a few professors who had congregated in the huge hall. I was asked to address the audience. Judging by my condition when I had this journey into the future, I could not even stand in front of ten students and address them coherently. Now, in that future, I was standing in front of thousands. I was petrified, to say the least.

"What is happening here?" I asked my Guardian.

Prepare Yourself

"You're going to lead them. So, prepare yourself." That was all he said to me.

I was confused and challenged. Why would anyone ever pick this shy and not-so-confident youngster to lead an organization of worldly-wise, creative, and boisterous students spread across several universities in Nigeria?

However, I had learned to obey and accept as gospel truth whatever Spirit revealed to me. So, I sat down in my contemplation chair and sang the sacred Word, as I had been taught — we will get to it later. As I sang this

Word, more understanding of the inner encounter came to me. I was going to become the national president of the Nigerian Universities Theatre Arts Students Association (NUTASA). That was a tough call, considering the responsibilities attached to that position. One of them was to organize the body of *Nutasaites* - as we liked to call ourselves - who were in their thousands.

The second major task was to organize what was the largest theatre festival in the world at that time. For about two weeks, several schools would gather at a single venue to perform plays, dance skits, and engage in debates and exhibitions. This festival attracted participants from around the world. Not less than ten thousand would attend. During this time, the national president had to organize and see to the transportation, accommodation, security, and welfare of thousands of delegates who had come from near and far. A tough job for a student; a tougher job still for a shy one.

Physical and Mental Preparation

Outwardly, I began to fraternize with those involved in the administration of the association to learn what was going on well and what was amiss. I also looked for the opportunity to get involved. The first opportunity was an invitation to sit on the parliament of the association. This body met a couple of times in the year to fashion out laws and review the group's activities from a legislative perspective. Here, I saw people I thought were years ahead of me in elocution, intelligence, and passion. I had to learn by watching them in action.

You Have Been Chosen

A year after the dream, two of my professors — Teju Olaniyan and Femi Folorunso — walked up to me to discuss the possibilities of OAU bidding for the presidential ticket of NUTASA. I was scared that reality had come too soon.

"We have been observing you for a while. We have chosen you as our candidate in the event of the school getting the slot." Teju Olaniyan, who later became Louise Durham Mead Professor of English at the University of Wisconsin–Madison, was the lead kingmaker.

"Sirs, there must be some other persons," I protested.

"Yes, there are," answered FF, who is now Development Officer, Creative Scotland. "There are other candidates, but you have been chosen. So, prepare yourself."

I stood still, speechless. My mind went back to the prophetic journey I had taken the previous year. The same words had been used by my Guardian Angel: "Prepare yourself."

I went back to the hostel to consult my Spiritual Experience Journal. I checked the entry containing the prophetic experience relating to the unfolding drama. I checked out the details, looking for pointers to help me handle the physical manifestation much better. This is one of the rites I had always done for years: writing my dreams and visions and then reviewing them from time to time. This had guided me for years since I was about 12. For me, it was fun looking forward to my dreams every night, writing them down either in the middle of the night or in the morning, and then reading the journal like a story-book. It was always exciting, and above all, instructive. It was a journey into my innermost being. I learned more about myself, the world around me, the spiritual realities, and the meaning of life from this journal.

I found two entries in the journal dating back to a few weeks before the dream. I had given Spirit a challenge: "I want to be the best in school. Remember I flunked my A-Levels. I want to go out more and be of service to life." These were two of the targets I had given myself and Spirit. I had completely forgotten about these entries. As we can see, Spirit never forgets. Spirit never reneges on agreements. The weak link in that chain from visualization to manifestation is us.

Reviewing the journal further, I looked out for pointers to guide me on how to respond to the offer that my professors had just made. Even though it had been shown to me, to actualize it in the physical world could still be as challenging as searching for a needle in a haystack. There was nothing in the journal entry that indicated the part to be played by my professors. So, common sense and inner guidance had to suffice.

I felt rather exposed and vulnerable realizing that what had been a perfectly kept secret between Spirit and me was now out in the world. My destiny seemed to have gone beyond me; it was now in the wide-open field. I had to do a mental readjustment to flow with the tide.

I went back to the kingmakers and thanked them for the offer. Of course, I could not have said to them, "I saw it in a vision about a year ago, and I've been working on myself, waiting for you guys to make this offer." That would probably have classified me as a weirdo. They would have disqualified me. Rather, I appreciated their good gesture and having a high opinion of me.

Dreams Come True

Less than a year later, I was at the University of Port Harcourt auditorium, standing before thousands of students and a few professors. I was introduced as the new president of NUTASA, having been ratified at an extraordinary caucus of the group's legislative body. I stood there, skinny, fragile, and shaking all over. I had two years to prepare but even if I had ten years, I would still have been nervous.

I thanked Spirit and my Guardian Angel for giving me a heads up regarding this herculean task. Ordinarily, I never knew I would ever be the president of such a large organization, even though I had shown more than a passing interest in knowing the future. I had the habit of picking a day in the future, or a better condition than I was in, and asking Spirit to show me the events of that day. Many a time, I was shown such a day, condition, or situation. There were also times I was shown events of other occasions outside the scope of my contemplation.

Create a Journal

Today, create a journal. You can use a notebook, a diary, or a folder on your phone or computer to write down this 21-day goal, the vision, dreams, messages, nudges, and other related experiences.

Note the Drama

You must also note any real-life drama that is being unfolded or staged by Spirit for your benefit. Throughout the day, think of receiving the solution or answer.

Write the Goal

When you are about to sleep, write down the goal. For example: "I want to see my future partner." or "I want to see the business or career I should pursue." Or "Should I marry Mr. XYZ?" And, if I do, "What will it be like?" It can be a health challenge for which you require healing or a miracle. Write it down as your goal within the next 21 days. Date and annotate it as **Day 1**.

Review the Day

As you prepare to sleep, sit in a chair, or lie in bed while you review all that happened during the day. If you wish, you can sing a Word for about 10 to 20 minutes, softly and solemnly. Later in the book, you will see these Words, out of which you can choose one. You can also choose another Word that is not on the list, if it works for you. Sleep with the expectation of having a remarkable dream. It may or may not come. Do not be bothered.

Relax completely and trust in Spirit as you doze off.

DAY TWO

OPEN YOUR EYES

Today, first, write down in your journal the dreams you had in the night. We will call it the Spiritual Encounter Journal (SEJ). You must have had a dream in the night, though the memory has become fuzzy; maybe you cannot even recall a shred of it. Whatever you can remember, please write it down, even if it is just a feeling, or an intuition that comes to you upon waking up. It has to do with the encounter you had in the Inner Worlds, which has turned hazy as you wake.

Review the Entries

Review the entries in the SEJ from the perspective of your 21-day goal. See if the dream, or intuition, or nudge, has any correlation with the goal. Yes, there is, but you might not be able to see it yet. Spirit is the Prophet and has dramatic ways It can use to pass across a message.

Normally, the beginning of a movie has a bearing on the whole theme and plot, but you cannot see it until possibly the middle or sometimes the end. Since we have agreed on 21-day duration, Spirit is aware of this. Furthermore, the Council of Saints, under the direction of your personal Guardian Saint or Angel, will be ready to play along; but you must be observant.

Develop the Power of Outer Seeing

Today, the task is observation. You must develop the

capacity of your outer seeing, which will, in turn, have a bearing on your Inner Eye, to see what is being shown in the Spirit Realms and capture as much detail as possible.

Habitually, we walk around half-blind and half-deaf to the beauty, pictures, and music with which life surrounds us. Most of us do not know the color of our car off-hand. Okay, you argue that? How about your plate number? You remember that? How about the exact color of the house you live in? The shape and the design? How about the color of your own eyes? You hesitate about that one, do you? Let us not bother you then about your spouse's and friend's. How about the name or message on the signboard at the junction of your street? You pass by it every day, but you are blind to it.

Capture Colors and Shapes

Today, you will open your eyes to capture the colors and shapes of life. What is the exact size and color of your TV, the seats, the clothes you are wearing, and the shoes? At the office or school, let us take in the color of our desk and the shape. Let us feel the wood, metal, or glass, and other details. How about the window blinds? The guys you meet at the bus station, what clothes are they wearing, and the design? How about their body shape, size, height, and skin tone? How do they smile and walk?

As you do this, which opens the outer eye broadly, you will realize life is more colorful, shapelier, and more beautiful than you have always seen or believed it to be.

At Day's End

At day's end, before sleep, write down any new details you notice that seem to have a bearing on your goal. For instance, about your wedding or your future partner, you probably remember seeing a sticker on a car that reads, 'Nurses Make Good Wives', or 'I Love Michael', or other things related to love, relationships, and marriage. Please write these down in the SEJ. It is part of the spiritual drama unfolding, scene by scene.

The same applies to other goals.

As I said earlier, some of these pointers and scenes will not make sense to you now but note them down. Their time will come.

Bedtime Technique

As you sleep, lie quietly in bed, and look at the position of the Spiritual Eye, which is where the two eyebrows meet. Tonight, your dreams will be clearer than usual. Get ready to write them even if you wake by 1 a.m. or 3 a.m. Leaving it until morning can make you forget it.

DAY THREE

OPEN YOUR EARS

As you wake, review your night dreams for about five minutes. Do not jump straight out of bed into the bath and your work clothes. That is like eating and standing on your head immediately after. You know what will happen.

Five minutes of reflection before your regular prayers or meditation is advised and appropriate. Write whatever you have learned from that quiet moment. Truth is, Spirit is speaking to us all the time, but we rarely listen.

Today, you will listen!

Yesterday, you opened your eyes; today, you will open your ears to capture and appreciate the sounds of life.

Have you ever noticed the pace at which you speak? The words you use? Are they kind or hurtful? Have you ever listened to your own laughter? How does it sound? What about sounds that surround you? News and music from TV and radio: how does the newscaster sound? How about your spouse, children, siblings, parents, co-workers, birds, car engines, waterfall, crickets, etc.? Note the sound. Note that you are part of this medley of sounds produced by nature, man, and other living things. It is like an orchestra.

Take cognizance of what people say around you,

even when they are not talking to you, but they are within earshot. Listen and make sense of it in relation to your life and Soul-Fullness goals. All life comes from the Source. Spirit is the medium the Source uses to communicate with us. Because all life is a stage, the drama is always exciting but subtle in meaning; so, you must listen carefully so as not to miss out on the action.

The Rewind Technique

At day's end, sit in quiet with your eyes closed and your attention placed at the Spiritual Eye. Breathe in and out gently and relax your body to eliminate the stress. Then do a rewind of the whole day, from now, back to when you woke up in the morning, just like you rewind a movie on your video player. The picture appears to be walking backward.

Try to remember sounds, words, and music that caught your attention. Does anyone or something make a strong impression on you? Is there a song or music that seems to stand out in your memory? Write it down in your journal, even if it does not appear to be directly connected to your 21-day goal.

THE FIRE

I was 18 when I had the baptism of the Holy Spirit. I had stopped going to church for four years because of the glaring hypocrisy of my church leaders and followers.

However, in my spiritual life, Angels were talking to me. I never told anyone. In the dream and in the conscious journey in Spirit, several Guardian Angels of black, white, Chinese, and olive skin colors came to me. They taught me the ways of God, the Heavens, and love. One of them, who had given his name as Paul, had asked me to read the Holy Books and tell him what struck me the most.

"Personal encounters with Spirit, the Voice, the Fire of God, and the meetings with the Angels," I replied. "And I want to experience it all," I had added.

Follow the Next Girl

One Saturday morning in February, a few months after this request, I was sitting at a school gate chatting with my friend, Mayor, when I heard a voice whisper, "Follow the next girl. Follow her to wherever she goes."

I turned around sharply to see who it was. There was no one apart from the two of us. To be certain, I asked Mayor if he had seen or heard anyone. There was no one in the vicinity for about a hundred feet.

"Hey man, what's startling you?" Mayor asked, looking at me with a puzzled expression on his usually smiling face.

Mayor had perceived the change in me, which was visible, though the experience was a spiritual one. There was no mistaking the voice. There was also no mistake about the source. I was used to seeing spiritual Light of different colors at the corners of my vision at rare moments, either while in bed, walking in the garden, or in deep thought. I was also used to hearing the voice of the Saints, either when in prayer or at that blurry, hazy moment before waking up from a dream.

Can Angels Lead Me Astray?

But this had a different tone to it. For one, I was surprised he would speak to me in the presence of a friend, in the middle of a conversation. I was used to being addressed by him in my quiet moments. Also, I was more than surprised I would be asked to follow a girl. That was not my idea of holiness. Angels were not supposed to lead me astray, talk less of commanding me to follow a babe! My dad would have turned livid with pure rage if he heard this.

But I knew the voice, and I had come to know the owner as a Guardian Saint of a pure heart. He could not possibly be leading me astray. He had been constant in my dreams for years before that time and had taught me a lot about God and life.

The Shy Lad

Yet, there was another problem. I was not a bold lad when it came to the issue of girls. To put it mildly, I was a shy and inexperienced 18-year-old with an overly strict father. So, why would anyone want to put me to test or subject me to public disgrace by asking me to follow a girl in the middle of a street, and in a neighborhood where I was well known?

To boost my courage, I told Mayor we should catch some fun by following the next girl to come our way. He knew how to talk to girls. But to worsen my plight, he declined.

"Sorry, my guy. I don't chase babes in this neighborhood. It is a holy ground for me. Their parents know me, and I don't want to invite any father's wrath."

Obey, I Must

I was on my own. Courage, I lacked. But obey, I must.

For ten minutes, no girl came our way. Then, Rosemary came along. Tall, self-assured, she took her steps like a seasoned model would, walking down the runway. She was about my age, but her unsmiling face when I said hello further intimidated me. She did not look at me, did not miss a step, neither did she answer me. Surprisingly, her apparently unwelcoming attitude helped to steel my nerves.

"Don't you know it's bad manners when someone says hello and you ignore them as if they've committed a crime against humanity?"

That seemed to activate something in her mind, and she missed a step. She turned in my direction for the first time with a look as lethal as a double-edged sword. "Don't you have better things to do than chasing after every girl you see?"

That was hurtful. For one, I had never summoned up the courage to go after a girl who was a total stranger, unless we were introduced. What she was accusing me of was far from the truth. However, she was right that here I was, chasing after a girl whom I had never seen or met in my life.

"For one, I don't chase after girls. You don't know me. Then, there is nothing wrong in saying hello, is there?"

She looked away and kept walking. I kept following. I was feeling highly embarrassed at this moment than I had ever been all my life. I wondered if I had actually heard a voice. And if I did, could it be the devil trying to put me to shame?

"My name is James. You can at least tell me your name if you want me to go away," I said, rather tamely. She did not answer me. She kept walking, or cat-walking to be precise, and I kept following. Soon, we got to a street junction. I reckoned she needed to turn left, either heading where she was going or trying to ditch me. I kept following; then, she began losing a little of her composure.

"Is this how you'll follow me all day?"

"Yes, actually that's my assignment; to follow you everywhere you go."

She smiled. "Even if I'm going to church?"

That was not a pleasant thought, but the Guardian Angel had given a command that must be obeyed. "Yes, I'll follow you to church or to the market."

"Then, let's go. My name is Rosemary."

"Lovely name." I took in a breath of relief. The tension abated a little, and I followed her to church where she had choir practice in preparation for Sunday service. While there, the pastor invited me to a three-day Holy Spirit revival. Immediately, I knew the reason for the whole drama.

The Fire and the Voice

On the following Wednesday, at about 8 p.m., I had my first direct contact with the Fire and the Voice of Spirit. It was like high-voltage electricity that knocked me into the wall. That came after I had seen one of the Guardians with a Golden Light around him, touching my forehead with what appeared like a little rod of light.

I had entered the Sacred Space and my life changed completely.

However, I lasted barely two weeks in that church because the experience was not a church thing. It was spiritual. I had to move on.

I have had similar experiences while chanting Buddhist and Hindu mantras, acting on stage in a one-man play, and at other times sitting alone in contemplation in my room, or while awake in the dream world. You can enter the Sacred Space depending on your readiness and the decision of Spirit.

Bedtime Technique

As you sleep, tell yourself to listen to and carefully watch all sounds, words, shapes, and colors in your dreams.

And please, when you wake, write down any dreams.

DAY FOUR

CLEAN UP THE PHYSICAL TEMPLE

Today, and throughout your 21-day journey into the future, you will embark on a cleanup of the body.

Many a time we deceive ourselves that what goes into the body cannot corrupt the Soul. Yes, it is true that Soul, our true identity, is above the vagaries of the physical world. But the progress or otherwise of Soul as a spiritual being is heavily affected by the body and the conditions surrounding it.

Just like a Car and the Driver

Let me be straight and frank. The body is like a car that you drive around town. Yes, you are not the car, but if it breaks down in the night, in the middle of nowhere, you will take an emergency trip to hell until you have sorted it out.

You do not want the car to subject you to such agony and torture. But that is what you get if you do not take good care of it. This includes regular trips to the car wash, periodic oil change, regular visits to the gas station, proper realignment, and other crucial checks.

When you take care of your car, your car will take care of you. If you take good care of your body, it will serve as a good vehicle that you, the spiritual individual, uses to experience life in the physical universe.

We know we should give it daily wash, feed it with good food and vitamins, exercise and realign it every night when we sleep. But some certain foods and drinks deaden the body's sensitivity.

Poisons

Alcohol, cigarette, marijuana, cocaine, substances that you have to smoke, excessive caffeine, pills that manipulate your thoughts and emotions outside your control, white sugar, white bread, excessively fatty foods, for instance, are high on the list of poisons that render the body less sensitive to the higher vibrations.

Just as sugar attracts myriads of ants, these poisonous substances open the spiritual centers of the body to invasion by negative entities that feed on the invisible radiations coming from these substances.

Like a Cell Phone

Our goal is to make the body do what a very good cell phone does for us. It picks up network signals, translates the content into sound (voice and music) and visual data (texts/pictures/light), so we can communicate effectively with the world.

In this case, we are using our body and brain to pick up and transmit thoughts, words, and ideas between the physical and the invisible realms we call Heavens. So, we must feed it with good food and prime it well so that signals from the Source can reach us loud and clear.

Higher Cleansing

As we make progress spiritually, we discover there are other foods and drinks we must drop. Later in the book, I will share my tough experiences with having to drop foods I used to cherish though they are regarded as healthy by nutritionists.

Spiritual Nutrition

But there is spiritual nutrition. A secret people are not aware of is that the Soul of the animal or plant colors the nature or vibration of the body, be it meat or vegetable. When you eat it, it, in turn, affects your behavior. For instance, I abstain from eating wild animals. Their nature, for the most part, is wild and incompatible with humans. Sheep, cow, goat, and other animals domesticated or reared by humans, have a mental and emotional nature that is compatible with and responds positively to humans.

SNAKE AND GOAT MEAT PEPPER SOUPS

A poisonous snake, for instance, will have its negative impact on the mind of the eater. I had a friend who suddenly developed a passion for snake meat pepper soup. I soon noticed that whenever we hugged, the next thing was to bare her teeth, make a hissing sound, and sink them into my chest. I first overlooked it, but when I began having bruises to show for these 'affectionate gestures', I discussed the issue with her and advised her to drop snake meat from her menu. She laughed it off. Well, I had a choice. I avoided getting too close to her. Soon, I noticed she began picking quarrels with neighbors, ending up a couple of times at the police station.

Randy as a Goat

My friend, Henry, used to have an uncontrollable sexual appetite. It worried him so much that he asked me for help. I noticed he was used to eating three to five plates of goat meat pepper soup every day.

When the wise man had said, 'as randy as a goat', he

was not just playing with words. Henry would have been seen as an active man in bed if he had a wife or steady partner, but as a single man with no steady girlfriend, he was a nuisance to himself and the whole town. He lined them up in his apartment, three to five a day.

"I need to be delivered from myself," he pleaded, sounding desperate.

I helped him review his diet and daily routine. Using the process of elimination, we were able to zero in on his excessive intake of goat meat pepper soup. In addition, we found out he threw in a bottle or two of alcohol to 'wash it down'.

For the majority, this combination of foods and drinks may or may not cause much of a physical or emotional upset to the system. But Henry was a man desirous of the company of the Saints. Anyone who desires the presence of Spirit must obey the stringent laws that govern that spiritual stratosphere where the Light and Music from the Source ebb and flow, bringing a large dose of Goodness, Mercy, Love, Wisdom, and Power. And to whom much is given, much is expected.

To Eat with the King

If you want to eat with the King, you must come to dinner looking clean, prim, and proper.

When we get closer to whom we were created to be — a spark of divinity — even our physical body changes in its makeup. The spiritual counterpart of our physical body changes in the amount of Light that it can hold. This invariably changes what the physical body can admit into itself. Like the phrase, 'level has changed', you have moved to a higher level of interaction with the Higher Power and life in general.

Food affects your body, mind, and emotions. Be watchful, and you will know what to keep or drop.

Caveat Emptor

A caveat here. The examples of foods and drinks I have given here are not to be strictly followed like a commandment. We are all different and operating at different levels of consciousness. Though I do not drink alcohol or eat snakes, I am not commanding you to drop them, but be watchful. Your dreams, emotions, and fitness level will tell you what is good or bad for you. A good barometer is to watch out if you have negative reactions of the physical, emotional, or spiritual kind between five to thirty minutes after a drink or twenty minutes to three hours after eating a particular food.

Above all, you must be honest with yourself. It is your life. You are responsible for your happiness, good health, illness, failures, and successes. Also, to rise above where you are at this moment, you must let go of the moorings, the attachments to the things, feelings, concepts, and beliefs that tie you to the place or situation you want to leave.

Freedom comes when we let go of the things holding us down and the things we are holding down. There is a price to pay before we can move into that larger, happier room. It is as simple as letting go of these poisons, albeit gradually.

Bedtime Technique

At day's end, review your activities for the day and write whatever stands out for you. Go to bed with the expectation of a revelatory dream.

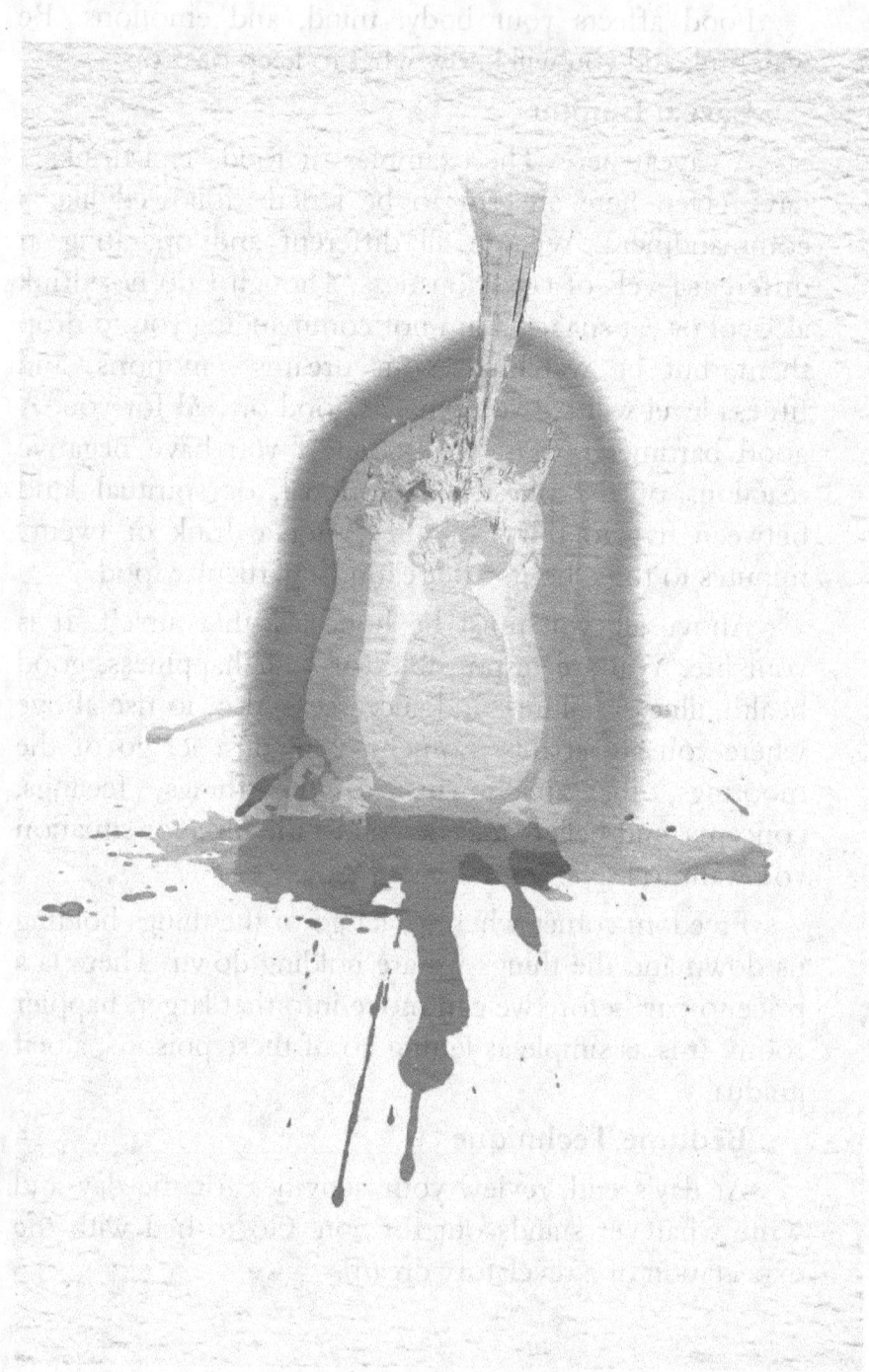

DAY FIVE

CLEAN UP THE EMOTIONAL TEMPLE

Man, as Spirit, has many bodies. In a house, there are many rooms. Each of the rooms has its specific duty, and this duty is what dictates its design.

The sitting room is a family place, a meeting point between visitors and the owners of the house, or the hosts. A kitchen is a place for making food, and the gadgets for producing fire and preserving items are kept there. The dining area is for eating food, while the toilet is for disposing of waste. The bedroom is for rest and lovemaking, while the study is for mental and intellectual work. The attic and basement are for storing what we do not need urgently.

Physical Body

The complex creature called man is built almost alike. The outer wall of the building is the physical body that we use for touch, taste, seeing, hearing, and smelling. Within the walls are other bodies or rooms.

Dream Body

Next is the emotional body, which is not just a concept but a real body. This is our dream body. Some call it the Astral body.

When we sleep, we leave the physical body and, with our dream body, we go to places in the dream world.

This is the first of the spirit bodies of man. It looks exactly like our physical body, but it is usually finer and younger in appearance. And, just like the five senses of the physical body, the dream body also possesses several faculties for experiencing life in the dream world.

The First Heaven

The first of this dream world is generally known as the First Heaven. For most people, when they die on Earth, this is where they go.

The First Heaven, just like this body, is a finer and much more lasting version of the physical world. There are places here that are so breathtakingly beautiful that most people want to stay for eternity. But it is just another school.

Senses of the Dream Body

Just like our physical senses pick up pleasant and unpleasant sounds, sights, tastes, etc., the dream body is exposed to feelings and emotions that can bring happiness or sadness. Some of these emotions translate to anger, lust, getting hurt easily, impatience, complaining about people, yourself, the weather, your job, house, children, the skin color of others, trying to harm others, suicidal feelings, wickedness, etc. These are feelings from the basement of the dream world.

Hell, Purgatory, Avernus

Just like the physical world has beautiful places and ugly places, so does the dream world. Many have referred to these unpleasant regions as 'hell', 'purgatory', or 'Seven Worlds of Avernus'. These dark places are filled with feelings and imaginings that create a block between us and the Source. We all are affected by the waves from these regions, whether we are awake or asleep.

Feelings from the 'Basement'

We must shun the feelings that come from the basement. There is scarcely any human being alive that has not taken a trip to these dark realms. Your nightmares are encounters you have with entities in the basement regions when you are asleep. Much of it is because of our thoughts, actions, and emotions of the past. That past could be this lifetime or previous ones. There are also mischievous entities in the dark regions looking for careless wayfarers to entrap.

Saint Paul, in the Christian Bible, admonishes that we should not let the sun go down on our anger. In other words, no matter the condition, any hurt emotion and anger should be forgiven and forgotten before nightfall. The spiritual implications include inescapable trips to the lower regions in our dreams if we focus on anger throughout the day and when we are going to bed.

Higher Emotions

The higher part of the emotional body gives us contentment, forgiveness, gratitude, healthy loyalty to family and nation, commitment and dedication to our children and partners. The thrill that comes from lovemaking emanates from here. This, however, is not the animalistic practice of taking advantage of the other person through rape, prostitution, sex for power and position, or sex with minors and animals. These are from the basement where the dark spirits rule.

Drugs and Demons

A link to **Day Four** and the food we consume: Drugs and alcoholic beverages help to open the channel in the emotional body, allowing the entities in the basement to invade the house.

Undue Attachment

Let me say a few words on nationalism and undue attachment to family, body, work, possessions, and faith. These feelings come from the emotional body. They can be uplifting, if moderate. But often, the dark spirits manipulate these emotions to block the pure Light.

When Loyalty Goes Wrong

Loyalty to our football club or political party easily becomes a tool for self-inflicted unhappiness and hating those who do not support us.

Loyalty to lovers and family becomes a source of worry and fears that create unhappiness and ill health.

Loyalty to the nation leads to hating and waging war on other nations.

Loyalty to our religion leads to bigotry and waging war on other children of Spirit.

An undue love of (and attachment to) our body and skin color can easily lead to hating other creatures of God who may have different shapes, sizes and pigmentation.

Know this: Whatever makes you hate, hurt, or look down on any other creature of God — including animals and plants — is an act of hatred directed at God. You cannot like some of the things the Source created and hate some. You do not have to sleep in the house of the wicked, but you must not hate them. Wish them well and go your way. God loves them as much as you.

Do Yourself a Favor

When we refrain from anger, hatred, envy, jealousy, and other negative emotions, we are doing only ourselves a favor. If you keep your house clean, plant lovely flowers in the garden, and keep it well-manicured, you enjoy the beauty and the sweet scent that accompany such an action.

Day Technique

Today, as you go about your business, purge your heart of feelings that bring fear, anger, and hatred to you and others. Spirit will not come into the house when it is polluted with poisonous gas.

Bedtime Technique

As you lie in bed, think of the events, people, places, and ideas that brought you unhappiness and how you have overcome them. The ones that you have not gotten rid of, say, "God, I don't need these feelings. Help me dissolve them in the River of Light." See yourself swimming in a river of sparkling water made of pure Light, and feel happy.

Sleep with a feeling of peace and freedom.

SPECIAL WORD ON SUICIDE

The first week of June 2018 witnessed several reports from America, Europe, and Africa of high-profile suicides. One of my close associates asked, "Why is suicide now becoming the way out of problems? Is there a spiritual prescription for those who are suicidal?"

Suicide has always been one of the weaknesses of the human mind. When the mind is fixated on deadlines, man invariably runs into dead ends repeatedly. A desperate pursuit of material gains and human relationships can never bring happiness. Yes, there will be some pyrrhic gains and so-called 'successes'. But they are not sustainable. Matter and tenuous social relationships will invariably depreciate.

The only source of happiness that is sustainable is the

cultivation of creative resources, joy, and peace within us. Love, charity, creativity, kindness, courage, humility, detachment from the desires of material and social objects and relationships bring to us freedom and happiness.

Help Is Available

But life in the physical world is far from being easy. Like I say, it is not a vacation. It is a school with the expected studies, tests, failures, and successes. But man is not alone. Help is available. The Guardians, Masters, Saints, and the Holy Spirit are right here as you read these words. All you need do is sincerely ask for help. But you must be honest and ready to accept the help that comes; otherwise, you will be further entangled in a giant hay of confusion.

First and foremost, realize that whatever happens is not the end of the world. Be it pleasant or unpleasant. Realize also, there is a blessing in every single action, event, moment, success, or failure. The difference between a spiritual infant and an adult is the ability to recognize these lessons and blessings, learn from them, and take advantage of them, respectively.

Do not fall into the negative trap of worrying about what people, family, society, journalists, bankers, investors, social media influencers and followers would say. Yes, it is exciting and thrilling to strive to be better than the next person and impress the whole world. But you must make yourself happy first before you can share it with others. The best way to do that is to do your best in every situation and let go of the rest.

The Invisible Neighbors

One secret that is unknown to many is that humanity co-exists with good and bad invisible forces. The evil forces are always seeking out people with a streak of aggression, anger, sadness, depression, and other emotional frailties. These negative-minded entities, like thugs and gangsters living in the invisible realms close to the Earth, feed on negative emotions as kids feed on candy.

Suicide Is Murder

Suicide is murder, the taking of a life. It is NOT an escape but an escalation of the problem. It is equivalent to breaking out of jail. It does not bring freedom. It only brings more troubles. Sooner than later, the inmate will be caught and will be back in prison but with extra punishment. Anyone who commits suicide has only broken out of jail, albeit temporarily. They will be back in no time as a newborn baby, plagued with the same challenges and nightmares they were not courageous enough to face the previous lifetime. And for taking a life they did not create, there will be extra penalties, extra troubles to face and overcome.

Temptation Determined by Capacity

Let everyone know this: No one is tempted beyond their capacity. God is not wicked. Life is not an accident. All is fair and in its rightful place. Secondly, challenges indicate an opportunity for growth, both materially and spiritually. A student who spends a whole year in class but never sits for tests and exams might as well have stayed back in their crib.

The Law of Returns

Ignorance of the unimpeachable Law of Karma and its flip side, the Law of Returns (reincarnation), is the bedrock of most of the troubles and confusion faced by the contemporary man and woman. We all have lived before. All that we have sown, we have returned to reap.

We return to pay our debts and collect our dues in the same environment and with the same people from the past. Phenomena such as deformities, privileges, talents, troubles, opportunities, and a strong attraction to people, places and things are coming from the memory bank of experiences garnered in past lives.

Therefore, in whatever situation we find ourselves let us realize we have earned it. Our concern should be how to move from this position we find unpleasant by placing ourselves in better conditions. We start by taking full responsibility for our thoughts, emotions, and actions. Let us not ever blame anyone for the condition in which we find ourselves. Rather, let us look for ways to get ourselves out of the quagmire, not how to sink deeper into it.

LETTER TO MY OLDER SELF

If you find yourself in an unpleasant situation that appears overpowering, do this: Write a **Letter to My Older Self**; address it to your future self about a year from today. You can write the letter on a sheet of paper, on your phone, or PC. Simply tell your future self about the problem you are facing. State why you think you got into this fix; state what you have done to extricate yourself from the problem, though all efforts have failed. Then ask your older self for help.

A good time to write is at bedtime, though it can be written at any time.

A solution will come in your dream. For some, solution comes even as they write. Whichever way, you will hear from your Older Self. Write down the dream or impression you get. Title it **Message from My Older Self**. Put it away and go about your life. A few days later, read the letter and the response. You will be able to see clearly. You can consult this letter as often as possible. You can also write as many times as possible to your Older Self.

I began using this technique while in high school. It has worked wonders. Put your heart in it. It works.

An Act of Charity a Day Keeps Troubles Away

Follow this with an act of charity daily. Charity, by the way, is not limited to giving money, food, and clothes to the needy. Forgiving yourself, forgiving others, saying kind words, encouraging others, making life a little easier for others are higher forms of charity. Do something for love. Love will find you. Even when life is dark and lonely, know that you are not alone.

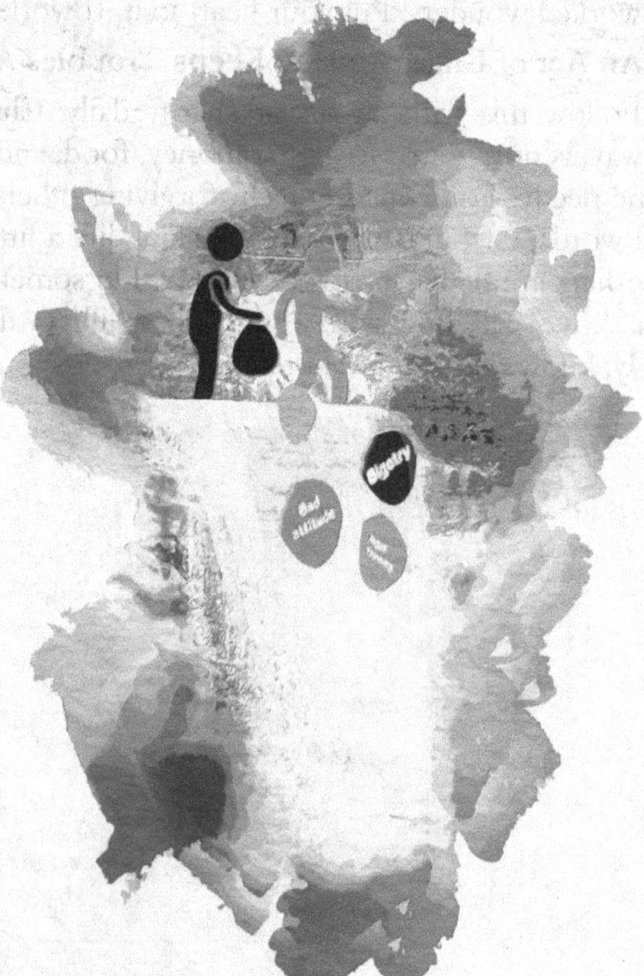
Bigotry
Bad attitude

DAY SIX

CLEAN UP THE MENTAL TEMPLE

The memory body and the thinking faculty called mind will be treated as one under the mental temple.

Today, we will get rid of attachment to ideas, thoughts, and memories that block the Light and Voice of Spirit.

These include pride, vanity, and self-aggrandizement, looking down on others, feeling superior, or feeling inferior to others. They include rigid thinking, unbending attitude, bigotry, unnecessary arguments, compulsion to win all arguments, and the desire to always be right.

Unpleasant Habits and Memories

Think about all ideas and attitudes that have led to unhappiness in the past. Why do you argue with people so much that you do not want to see their faces ever again? How about the memories from childhood, high school, and former relationships that bring you unhappiness? Dump them in the River of Light.

Habit Replacement

Consciously replace them with self-confidence that does not stray into the unwholesome territory of superiority complex or arrogance. Cultivate humility, contentment, appreciation of others, gratitude, and charity. Allow others to have their own opinion and faith.

Do not dominate discussions. At the same time, be alert and aware of those who want to enslave your mind and spirit with their ideas and emotions. This could be the ploy of the deceptive and lying spirits that dwell in the dark regions, looking for careless and carefree minds to entrap.

FAKE PROPHET; FAKE SPIRITS

I was 17 and overdue for admission into the university. My family was divided on the school I should attend and what course to study. We lived in Lagos. The University of Lagos was the unanimous choice of my sisters and uncles. I was not excited about that because I knew life would be just like I never left home, with everyone barging in on my privacy and making every decision for me. I knew a boy becomes a man only when he can make his own decisions and take whatever responsibility that goes hand in glove with them. Schooling too close to our home would keep me a boy for a long while.

Also, the family wanted me to study Law or Political Science. I wanted English or Literature in English because I knew I came to this world to write, among other things. What I was to write, I did not know, but I wanted to hone my skills and abilities while discovering the subject to write about.

The conflict at home was real and divisive, especially whenever exams into colleges were approaching. Since I would not budge, my brother suggested I go see his friend, a self-styled prophet to whom I will assign the sobriquet 'BJ' in this story. My brother had a strong faith in this guy as a prophet because they had had a couple of dealings regarding spirits and other issues. Since I was three years old, I had been conscious of the presence of spirit beings. I also knew there were evil or deceptive spirit beings that lurked in the shadows, waiting to trap gullible minds.

I told my brother I was not seeing any prophet. What stopped me from seeing my own future by myself? After all, God created me as It created the so-called prophets.

My brother referred to my attitude as childish arrogance. I did not like that; so, I agreed to see the famous prophet. Before I went, I prayed about it. In the Spirit, I was told by my Guardian Angel to go see the prophet but that I should put him to the test. I did both.

My aim was to find out the course God had chosen for me and the school to apply to. I first did not know how to put him to test until I got to his house and he asked me to go buy candles and writing paper. He instructed me to write on a plain sheet of paper my desired schools and courses. This was not how I thought a prophet operated. Was he not supposed to know everything? Or could he not just ask the spirits to tell me or show me the future? This guy was asking me to supply the spirits vital info.

"These guys are ignorant," I said to myself. "The Holy Spirit sees and knows everything. It won't ask for a helping hand from a teenager in need."

Tricking the Spirits

Then I got a nudge from Spirit to write the schools and courses, but I should mismatch them. For instance, OAU did not offer Mass Communication, but I wrote it as an option. I mixed up all the options and folded the paper, and placed it in the middle of the seven candles he had lit in a circle on the floor.

BJ never touched the paper. He only read from his book of incantations. I was bold, but my heartbeat raced as I felt the spirits enter the room. To counter them, I centered my thoughts completely away from the paper, what was on it, and the invocations. Rather, I focused on my Guardian Angel, whom I saw as a being of Light entering the room, wrapping me in a holy embrace.

In addition, I silently called upon my mom to join me in the room. For more than a year since she passed on, I had regular interactions with her both in the Heavens and in the physical. A few times we had met in the dream, and other times she had made appearances in my room. I knew she was aware of all that was going on in my life. I also knew she had a good aura that could protect me from harm. Summoning her to shield me from spirits that were not particularly holy was just in order.

"If they are evil, don't let them touch me. Don't let them deceive me," I said to her. In a short while, I had a warm feeling around my neck and shoulders like someone hugging me from behind. I knew I was in the good hands of my mom, my Guardian Angel, and Spirit.

While BJ was doing his thing, my eyes were half-closed. But I could see every move he made, and I heard every word he chanted. I did not understand the language, but I could make out every word. I was recording every detail for careful analysis later.

The Fake Miracle

After few minutes, the incantations ended. 'Prophet' BJ asked me to pick up the paper, unfold it, and read. I did as he directed. I was amazed at what I saw on the sheet of paper. I discovered that an invisible entity had marked two schools with what looked like charcoal and had written an instruction that I should fast for a day and give a particular amount of money to beggars.

The last two were not new to me. I regularly did that without any prompting. Sometimes, I would have the nudge or see me doing so in my dream; I would go out deliberately to render some service without reward or give money to beggars or any other person in need. Fasting was not always far from my schedule. My mom had brought us up on periodic 21-day fasts at least two or three times in the year, in addition to the Christian annual lent of 40 days. The rigor was not always a welcome idea, and my dad did not go along with it.

But the spirits had failed the tests. The invisible hand had marked and approved school and course combinations that did not exist. I did not tell BJ about this grand failure.

My father's common saying came to mind here: "Satan has power but can't offer anyone salvation." Apparently, BJ and his errant spirits had the ability to display magical phenomena. Yes, but they were ignorant goons.

Because of this power to make things appear from thin air, and mysterious but legible writings, many people fell for BJ's claims. They subsequently surrendered their heart and mind to the lowly but mischievous dark entities. I would have fallen for their tricks too, if I had not had the support, guidance, and protection of Spirit and the spiritual forces. It was a narrow escape.

Total Failure

BJ wanted to know if I got the answer and solution to my problem. I nodded yes, with a self-indulgent smile. BJ immediately began telling me some of his other services and achievements. I promised to be back for more consultation. I did not tell him that he and his spirits were a total failure.

My brother was also eager to hear about his friend's prowess. All I told him was that his friend had invoked the spirits and they wrote some schools and courses for me. I never said a word to my brother about everything that had transpired. He would not have been happy to know that I tricked his beloved prophet and the spirits. I did not want him to hate BJ. Why? I knew my brother still had a lot to learn from BJ. I did not want to come between them.

As for me, I had gone beyond the stage of being carried away by psychic phenomena. As Saint Augustine of Hippo posited, there is a major difference between appearance and reality, between phenomenon and the *noumenon*. However, the line between them is very thin and almost imperceptible. It takes a discerning Soul to tell them apart. It is the difference between falsehood and truth, between illusion and reality.

After this encounter with the deceptive spirits, I was determined, more than ever before, to see this aspect of my future. So, I challenged my Guardian Angel. "I want to see my future right now!"

Nemesis

Later, I will narrate what I saw in my trip to the future. As for BJ, he lost his mind a few months afterward. One early morning, he had stared into a well, but instead of seeing water, he saw a raging fire. He screamed out of shock and was never the same again until he was incarcerated in a popular psychiatric hospital outside Lagos. Years later, after I had finished my university education, I met him. He was now healthy and sober.

"I've given up that business of spirits. Now I rely on God only."

Good for him.

Bedtime Technique

Today, go to bed while reviewing your day and the things you saw, felt, and thought that gave you freedom from all ideas, thoughts, and persons that erect a block between you and Spirit.

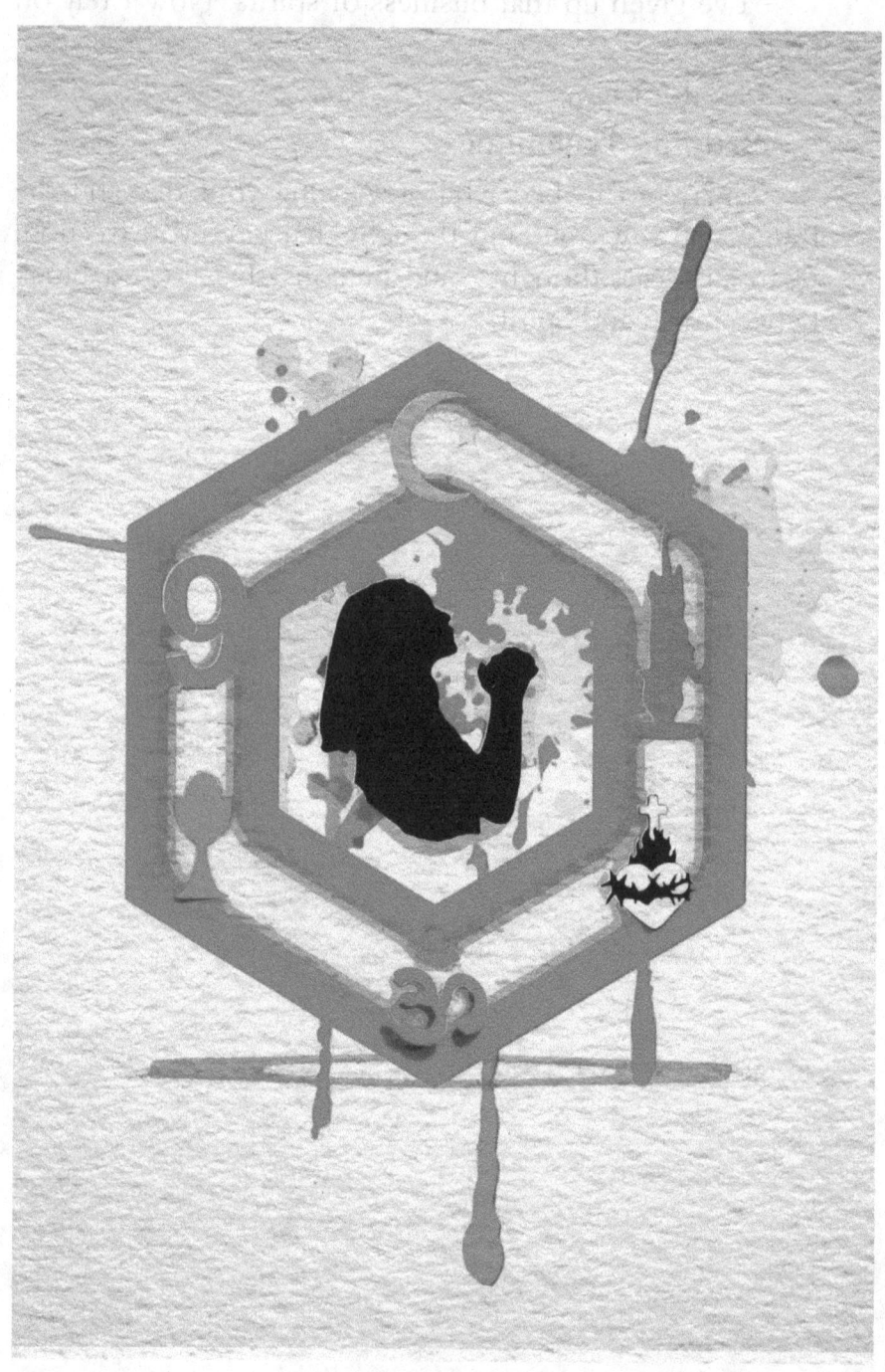

Tosin King James

DAY SEVEN

DEVELOP LANGUAGE OF COMMUNICATION WITH SPIRIT

Spirit has myriad ways of talking to each one of us. Why is that so? We are all unique, different units in the Heart of God. Soul is unique, individual, special, and incomparable. We are God's breath, God's Spirit.

In life, language or mode of communication includes words, sounds, letters, hand signs, and parts of the body positioned in a particular way. It involves numbers and symbols, which, by agreement, mean a particular concept, thought, feeling, emotion, or memory. The symbol of a cross stands for Church or Christ, while the symbol of a star and crescent stands for Islam. Red light at a crossroads means 'stop!'

As it is between us, so it is regarding our language of communication with Spirit. It also uses symbols, sounds, words, letters, numbers, light, colors, shapes, and dramatized scenes and events to give us a message of understanding and of prophecy.

Dream Symbols of Joseph

In the story of Joseph in the Bible, or Yusuf in the Quran, he dreamed and saw the future. In that future, his elder brothers would bow before him. It was not plainly told to him; rather, symbols were used by Spirit to represent the actual meaning.

Most of us are used to symbols that represent a thought or feeling. The apple or shape of the heart drawn on paper, or cast in gold or jewelry, means love. It does not mean hatred unless the heart is broken in two or the apple is rotten.

Develop Your Spiritual Morse Code

So, today you will develop your own Morse code, or the language you will be using to communicate with Spirit. Let us rephrase that slightly: You will develop one or two symbols and a few other means of communication, which you would like to agree with Spirit as the means to use to reveal information regarding the 21-day goal you are embarking on.

For example, answer to "Should I say 'yes' or 'no' to Michael's proposal?" could be given to you via the traffic lights. You can say, "If it's all green, then it means 'yes'. A single red can mean 'no'." A bird chirping by the window at bedtime can be agreed to mean 'yes, you're on the right track'.

Develop your own prophetic code, but do not be rigid. You must open your eyes and ears because Spirit cannot be limited. Let me give two instances in which Spirit revealed the future using two completely different means and styles of communication.

VANESSA

I was seriously thinking of entering a long-term relationship with Vanessa (not her real name). She liked me a great deal, and I felt the same way about her. But I decided to ask for Spirit's opinion, insight, or prophecy.

This was a habit I cultivated after I left the university. The average person never thinks of asking for inner guidance *before* entering a relationship. Most of us are directed by what our eyes can see in terms of looks and outward appearances or family and social status. We usually start dating first before we ask, "God, is s/he the right person for me?" That is like eating food and then calling the dietitian to know if what you ate was good for you. It is human nature.

I was not different from the average youngster. I was looking for love at first sight, like most people. I was moved largely by what I saw, heard, and felt about a lady. But what the sight perceives can be deceiving. So, after a few bruises to the heart, I learned to ask for inner guidance.

In this case, I was just a little better than most of my friends. I was already in the relationship; I felt the need to ask for guidance only because the relationship was getting serious. While I asked for guidance, I was hoping for a 'yes' from God.

The Oracle Speaks

This Sunday afternoon, I sat alone in my living room singing the Word solemnly. My eyes were open, riveted on a spot on the wall about five feet away. Just after three minutes, it appeared as though the plain wall had turned into a movie screen. On it was written a symbol, bold and large enough for me to realize it was Vanessa's birth date turned upside down. Let us use 25 as an example. I was in the habit of writing this number, instead of her name, whenever I made an entry about her in my diary.

I stared and waited, listening for any other images, words, or sounds. But that was it, just the lady's birth date written upside down. After a few seconds, it slowly faded and the 'movie screen' became the plain wall it always was.

Going Against the Oracle

I knew the meaning. It was clear, but it was hard to accept because I had developed feelings for her.

What did I do? I went ahead to date her! I knew Spirit never lied, but I wanted to see whether occasionally I gave wrong interpretations to these prophetic messages.

So, what happened? It started out as love at first sight. Soon enough, the worms in the rotten apple invaded my mouth from the first bite of the forbidden fruit. The relationship turned my life upside down. I lost almost everything, from material possessions to peace of mind. Lucky I was to have escaped with my life and sanity intact.

THE EAVESDROPPER

The second story is that of a friend. Early morning, he was on his way to the house of a business partner on appointment. He was to pick up a check and head to the bank. It was a Friday, and he was broke. All he had on him was just enough to buy gas into the tank to take him to the other guy's house.

As a habit, he said a prayer, "God, guide me and show me Thy ways." Just as he finished and was turning into the gas station, he saw two young men by the curb talking in loud voices.

The Bystanders

"If you go to his place now, you won't meet him," one of them said, apparently talking about a common friend.

"Why not? Where can he be this early morning?" the second man challenged.

"He's not at home; that much I know."

Overhearing this conversation, my friend felt a chord pull within him. These two persons he did not know neither were they aware of him. Immediately, he had the spiritual understanding that this was a prophetic message for him from Spirit.

He promptly pulled over into the gas station and called his friend's cell phone. The number was switched off. That was unusual. He sat there in the car, trying the number repeatedly and getting the same response. After a while, he decided not to buy gas and to turn back. He did, relying on Spirit as a faithful friend that is never wrong.

About an hour later, he got a call from his friend. The man had received an urgent call at dawn that his mom was critically ill in another town, which was several hours away. He was on the road and would not be back until Sunday evening.

My friend was not happy at the turn of events, but he was grateful for Spirit's help that saved him from spending his last cash and embarking on a fruitless journey.

Spirit Is a Dramatist

Spirit is always talking to us once we have agreed to communicate with the Source. But we hardly hear or listen. A good start is to develop a language of communication. Let us write the code or symbols down in our journal. But let us not be rigid. Spirit is a dramatist. It uses dramatic symbols, events, and words to give Its messages.

DAY EIGHT

GRATITUDE I:
THANK GOD FOR LIFE

Today — better done on a Sunday — you will begin a cycle of seven days during which you will send love and gratitude to Spirit on different areas of life, on different days.

Sunday is dedicated to giving love and thanks to God for Creation. As you go through the day, focus on every aspect of the Creation that you can see, hear, and feel. While at it, see the part you play in this eternal drama called life.

Link between Gratitude and Soul-Fullness

What has gratitude got to do with healing, seeing the future, or receiving messages from Spirit? Everything. Gratitude is an act by which we open the spiritual heart for Love to flow from Spirit, through us, to another Soul or object. It is a powerful spiritual tool for opening the gateway between the Heavens and us. It is the password that grants us access to the portal of boundless blessings.

Waves of Light and Music

Love is not a physical substance or product. It cannot be bottled and put up for sale. It only exists when we open our hearts for it to flow through. It comes in waves of Light and Music from the highest Heavens, down through the mind, memory, and emotional bodies of man, eventually reaching the physical. In the physical body, it passes through the heart area (in the aura) and radiates in beautiful crimson color all around us. At a higher level however, the color changes.

Love Radiation

When we meet or are in the presence of a loving person, we feel this person is 'glowing' or 'shining'. What happens is that our spiritual body/heart is sensitive to the love radiation coming from the other person's heart and spiritual body.

Love Is Magic

Without love, we feel dead. Without love, even an otherwise beautiful environment or person will feel dead. That is why it is possible to be surrounded by all the expensive and glittering things of life and still remain unhappy and unfulfilled.

How to Generate Love

The simple trick or technique for generating love is gratitude. Be grateful to Spirit for life, for the mountains, the seas, the skies, the trees, the air, and all the sounds and music that you hear. Be grateful to Spirit for creating you and all the other countless Souls, be they human, animal, plant, or mineral.

Throughout today, do not ask for anything from Spirit, but be grateful. All is beautiful, all is good and lovely, and all is well. Just be thankful.

Sing, 'Thank You'

You can sing or chant, 'Thank You' or 'Thank HU', either out loud or silently. Place your attention on an aspect of Creation and see how it has enriched your life, then chant, 'Thank You'. When you do this properly, you will feel a wave of happiness, love, and peace coming from the top of the head and through the heart. You will feel energized.

Past, Present, and Future Exist in Spirit

The future is an event, place, time, or object that exists in Spirit, the same as the present and the past. If we are not grateful for the whole of Life — containing the present, past, and future — how do we gain entrance into the Chamber of Prophecy, the key to alchemy which exists in the Second Heaven?

Bedtime Technique

At the end of the day, lie in bed with your eyes closed and your attention placed at the Spiritual Eye. Think back to the whole day and how your life has been made richer by this prayer of gratitude to Spirit for all life.

As you sleep, you will be taken into the First or Second Heaven to see, hear, and feel Creation at a higher and grander level.

Tonight, your journey in the dream world will be richer and more beautiful. The future or change you seek will likely be revealed to you in vivid pictures and sound. Write down whatever you see and hear in your Spiritual Encounter Journal.

DAY NINE

GRATITUDE II:
THANK GOD FOR YOUR POSSESSIONS

The second day of the gratitude technique will focus on all your material possessions.

You will focus your gratitude on the things you have. Why is this an important spiritual technique? You are seeking information from Spirit on how you can improve your life in the present so the future will be much better. A happier marriage, a better paying job, a healthier body, or a bigger house. But where will these things come from? From Spirit, of course.

How about the things you have now that you believe are not enough or inadequate? Of course, they are from Spirit.

You should appreciate all the big and small blessings Spirit has given you for you to enter the realm of abundance. Abundance, they say, flourishes in the life of a grateful heart.

SOUL JOURNEY TO MY FUTURE COLLEGE

It is quite easy for an 18-year-old who is desperately seeking admission into a university, and whose mom died in her prime just a few months earlier, to think he has nothing in the world. Yes, it is natural to feel short-changed by the world and God, especially. But that would be a mistake.

That was how I felt after the encounter with the fake prophet, BJ. As I left him, I was not in any way nearer my goal of gaining admission or knowing my course of study and the school to apply to. I had no mom to go home to, to discuss the problems with. I could not discuss it with my brother because of his unshakable faith in BJ and his ilk.

Encounter with Mom in the Spirit

So, I had to go within and commune with my Guardian Angel and my mom. After mother's death, I had had the privilege of visiting with her in the Heavens where she was now living. The visits brought me relief and hope. She knew I was worried and feeling abandoned.

I had seen her a few times, and her form was startling to my Spiritual Eye. Before she died, she had put on some weight, especially in the waist area. But when she appeared to me, she was trim, looking like an 18-year-old young woman with her skin glowing. It took some spiritual adjustment to my mind and emotions before I could accept her as my dead mom.

"Why did you have to die?" I asked her, with all the passion I had bottled up all this while. "It's not fair for you to leave like that. Why did you have to die, leaving us all alone in the world?"

"It Shall Be Well"

"I am not dead, so don't cry. Stop worrying; it shall be well," she had assured me.

While she was talking with me, one of the Guardian Angels was standing by. He never intruded but stood watching, reassuring.

The meetings with my mom were always at the instance of the Guardian Angels. That is one of the reasons they are called guardians. They facilitate encounters between others and us, either here or in the Heavens. They make sure these encounters are for our spiritual growth, nothing harmful or threatening.

Reasons to Be Grateful

That evening, as I lay in bed to review the events of the day and the past year, I discovered I had much to be grateful for. I had just escaped the trap of deceptive spirits that would have led me down a deadly and destructive trail had I fallen for the magical displays of BJ. What wiser and older people had fallen for was what I had deflated like a fragile balloon. I even had fun in the process. I had graduated from high school with the right grades. I was healthy. I had the protection of Spirit and my Guardian Angel. To crown it all, my dear mom was sending me love from the Heavens.

Why was I not grateful? I had so much to be grateful for. Rather, I locked myself in my room moping, hating my life, and blaming God and everyone I ever met.

I began to fill my heart with gratitude to God for my life. This lifted the darkness that had shrouded my heart for about a year. With this lightness, I drifted off to dreamland.

Soul Journey to OAU

Moments later, I became aware of being in an expansive place, heavily wooded with tall buildings designed beautifully. I was walking down a well-paved road surrounded by many young people I realized were students going to and from lectures. A few rode cars and bikes, while most walked. There were painted taxis and a few buses. The air was cool, with a pleasant scent. There were several almond trees lining the roads. The trees were covered with ripe fruits, the source of the sweet scent.

I knew I was at a university, but its name, I did not know. The students were in their thousands. The ambience was unmistakably intellectual. I could see lecture halls and theaters. The orderliness and neatness did not escape my notice. Two qualities I had come to associate with scholarliness.

In physical life, I had perfected the practice of looking around wherever I went, taking in the details, colors of the environment, and the names on signboards. It helped me to identify and recall locations and events related to them. So, I looked around to see if I could see a sign, but there was none. This was not a regular street or road.

Fausa

While I was wondering about the place, I saw a tall, slim lady coming in my direction. Soon, I recognized Fausa. She hugged me and asked if I had gained admission into the school. I replied that I would soon be coming there to study. We hugged once again. Suddenly, I could not see her anymore but became aware of a gentleman who had, all along, been beside me but was not visible during the conversation. This was my Guardian Angel who had arranged this trip to the future.

I woke up and wrote down the experience. While at it, I realized I did not know where Fausa was schooling. We had been mates in high school. She was a brilliant and focused student. She made all her papers and got into university the following year. I knew this encounter contained the answer to my worries. The university I should attend was the same where Fausa was now a student. The name, I did not know, but that should not be a problem.

I sought out one of my friends who knew where Fausa was schooling. It was Obafemi Awolowo University. That was it. I was going to apply to that school. So, I did and was admitted without a fuss.

Law of Silence

I had to keep this information to myself. One of the spiritual secrets of prophecies and your personal destiny is the Law of Silence. Except otherwise directed by Spirit, you must keep the communication between you and Spirit your personal affair. It is not to be revealed to anyone, no matter how close they are to you. Revealing it before it manifests can make it not to happen or you may be left with a poorer version.

Gratitude, Key to Revelation

In this revelation, you can see how gratitude led to a revelation. You can also see how Spirit sometimes uses dramatic techniques to reveal vital truth to you.

DAY TEN

GRATITUDE III: THANK GOD FOR WISDOM

As you wake up today, write down your dream and the understanding you get from meditating on it in the morning.

Say your regular prayers but, in addition, thank God for wisdom. Today, our goal is to tap into the pool of Spirit's Wisdom. Wisdom is an aspect of what we gain when we are linked up with Spirit. To take advantage of this blessing, we must accept and acknowledge the numerous gifts of wisdom we have received from Spirit that helped to improve our life.

We Take Spiritual Gifts for Granted

We take these gifts for granted because we think our brains and the intelligence we apply to an apparently simple act, like going to the bathroom, walking the dog, dating, making babies, or taking complex decisions like running an office or a business, belong to us.

Intelligence Is Not Ours

"I used my intelligence to solve that problem," we often boast. But is intelligence or wisdom ours?

In our vanity, we are eager to judge others as not wise enough compared to us. But, just like money and all material possessions, we own nothing. Not even intelligence. It all emanates from the Source. All the part we play in the matter is to consciously make ourselves an unselfish and open channel for this Light of Spirit to pass through and manifest as intelligence when applied to situations and problems.

Be Humble and Appreciative

If we want more of this Light to shine through us, then we must be humble and appreciative of the Source. Spend today being grateful for all the wisdom you have ever applied. And the one you are applying now. Reading a book or listening to a reading, understanding the thoughts, emotions, and actions involved is a practical example of the Light of Spirit flowing through you. The Light is the bearer of intelligence. Acknowledge it, and more will come. What you seek will come when you align yourself with this Light.

SPIRITUAL HELP IN CLASS

I was now a final year student, and the heat was on. Apart from the herculean task of making sure my grades never dropped as the leading student in my class, at the same time I had to oversee a national association of students while planning what was the biggest student theatre festival in the world at that time. In addition, I had to publish a high quality, annual journal that circulated round the member schools and several culture establishments. And, of course, we had to raise funds for all these projects simultaneously.

The fact that I had to travel round the schools and miss several classes did not help matters in the least. I was stretched to the limit and was close to snapping.

My Spirit Companion

My succor was in Spirit that bathed me constantly with Its Light and the Celestial Music. I sang the Word quietly to myself wherever I went. I surrendered completely to Spirit for guidance, wisdom, and strength. I regularly received these gifts. Soon, we were being directed to those who could help us. A notable publisher offered to print thousands of copies of the magazine free of charge after another publishing firm had typeset it free. These charitable people were way above our social rank, and we had never met them. The only person we had in common was Spirit, whom we relied on to lead us to them. And It sure did.

This day, I was returning to school from one of those excruciating trips that drained me of water and strength. On the bus, I was silently singing the Word, full of gratitude to God for wisdom and direction, without which we would have achieved nothing. Suddenly, my mind went back to my abandoned lectures in school and my final year project. I must not fail. My dad would never forgive me. He did not send me to school to manage a students' association at the expense of my studies and degree.

Urgent and Compulsory Test to Come

While doing this practice of gratitude, my awareness opened and expanded enough to know that I would have to write an urgent and compulsory test back on campus. What it was going to be all about, I did not know. This is an aspect of prophecy I was quite used to at the time. It comes like a subtle nudge telling you things to come. It is so subtle it is easy to pass off as a feeling or just an idea.

Receiving this prophetic insight, I asked my Guardian Angel what it was going to be and how I could prepare myself for it. After asking this question, I remained silent in my mind and emotions. Most times, our minds and emotions are so noisy and jumbled that we can scarcely hear the Silent Voice within. We are too busy concentrating on the problem to be aware of the Voice whispering to us a solution to the same problems that have put us in a quandary.

A regular practice of going silent, quieting the mind and emotions will go a long way to help us rise above the confusions associated with the human mind and social life. It is good to think and debate issues in our minds. But it is better to enter a Silent Mode after debating the issues. It is at that moment that the Higher Power can intercede with useful directions, nudges, hints, visions, or prophecy that will bring a lasting solution. Man is never without help; we are never left alone in our troubles. But are we listening?

It is a paradox that hidden in every problem is the solution. Underneath conflict and war is peace and reconciliation. Every question has an answer intricately woven into it. In every situation is a hidden ladder to help us rise above it. But we must be silent, open the Inner Eye, and open the Inner Ear, watch and listen.

Secret in the Newspaper

I was listening. And the Silent Voice floated in like a whiff of smoke, like a cat on silent feet.

"Read the newspaper and look out for an article on Europe." The voice was clear and matter of fact.

I looked around me on the bus. Not far from me was a guy holding the day's edition of *The Punch* newspaper. I asked to read it. Eagerly, I flipped through the pages, looking for the article on Europe. There it was towards the end. It was a story culled from *The Times* of London. The writer argued that the decay in socio-economic sectors of Europe had an intrinsic effect on the cultural values of the people. I read it twice to commit the argument to memory. Even at that, I could not see how the article was connected to any of my courses.

I soon got to school, and I had a choice to head for the hostel considering my tiredness or go to the department to know what had been happening in my absence. Inwardly, I asked for direction.

Spirit said, "Go to the Department."

I took a short walk to the Institute of African Studies, where Dramatic Arts was located. During the walk, I sang the Word while surrendering whatever was coming into the hands of Spirit. This helped lessen the pounding of my heart. Something challenging was about to happen. But was I not just returning from several challenging and daunting assignments? So, why worry?

Battle of Wits

I got to the Department to see my classmates all seated in class before one of the most difficult of our professors. I joined the class while searching the faces of some of my closest friends. All I got were stony stares that conveyed nothing but trouble. What could be going on here? I soon found out.

There was a battle of wits which the professor had just won. It was a class on European drama of the 19th century. He had thrown a question to the class but, as usual, my mates turned it into a joke. No one gave him an answer. Everyone was jesting instead.

This seemingly unserious habit of my classmates used to unnerve me when I first got admission into the school. I was raised in a very strict environment. If you want to play, play hard. When it comes to work, you must be serious. But when you bring together many youngsters who are learning to be actors, writers, directors, and producers, sometimes seriousness was seen as uncreative. It took me a long time to adjust to the endless clowning in class.

This attitude had infuriated the no-nonsense professor who promptly ordered an unscheduled test. The class protested and insisted on not writing the test. This further exacerbated the conflict. To assert his supremacy, he not only insisted on the test but vowed it would be 40 percent of the marks for the whole course.

To say the least, the whole class was like a boiling cauldron filled with fire-spitting dragons.

Gratitude

I sat down and quietly sang the Word, first thanking God for two consecutive prophecies that had come to pass within the hour. Without the inner guidance, I would most likely have been sleeping in my bed back at the hostel. Secondly, I had a fair idea of how to answer the test with what I had garnered from the newspaper article.

Asking for Help

Because it all comes from Spirit, I had to ask for guidance on how to write the test. Silently, I sang the Word and got help. I began with three paragraphs, summarizing the socio-economic and cultural status of modern Europe. I ended by linking it with the theatre of the 18th and 19th centuries. After writing a page and a half, I had nothing more to say. I dropped my pen and put my head on the table. The professor asked if I was done. I submitted my paper while my colleagues were still scratching their heads.

To my consternation, the professor began marking my paper right there. Within two minutes, he was done.

"You guys must be finished by now," he prompted the class. Most of them reacted with anger.

"You're distracting us, Sir. After all, it's one hour you

gave us for the test."

The professor pointed out that I had since finished. Many of them said that was my business and not theirs. They were insinuating that I must have written rubbish to have submitted so early, coupled with the fact that I was absent from school for almost ten days. I shared their feelings about the quality of my answer. But the biggest shocker of the day was to soon follow.

It Is a Miracle!

The professor picked up my paper, raised it up for all to see. From the back, I craned my neck to see my scores.

"When you finish, all of you must read this. This is how to answer questions."

There was complete silence in the class. Even my jaws dropped. I had scored an A! I could not believe it. This was a professor who used to boast that A was for God and B was for the Angels. Well, for the first time, I agreed with him. This test and the answer I gave belonged to God, and God got Its due!

The Pool of Wisdom and the River of Light

The Pool of Wisdom emanates from the River of Light which contains all wisdom, intelligence, understanding, guidance, direction, and nudges. Without these, even the simplest task of adding 2 + 2, talk less of dating, building a house, child-rearing, or driving a car, would be utterly impossible.

Bedtime Technique

Let us go to bed with gratitude, quietly singing HU, or another spiritual Word. When we sleep, Spirit will be waiting to give us more of Its Wisdom from the Second Heaven where the Chamber of Prophecy exists.

DAY ELEVEN

GRATITUDE IV:
BE GRATEFUL FOR THE LOVE IN YOUR LIFE

This morning, you must have recorded a remarkable dream or insight you had during the night. It all has a bearing on your life. You probably had a dream about a loved one or about your love for someone, a job, or a project. Attention is on your love balance sheet. Are you giving more than you are taking, or are you demanding more than you are ready to surrender?

Our Problems Are Rooted in Love

Truth is, the problems, worries, and fears we have are all rooted in love. We have all taken more from life than we have given. We are surrounded by life we have grown accustomed to. We never question how this life, which we enjoy or dislike so much, got here.

Imagine for a moment how all these things we desire got here. Ask yourself, how did I get here? Ask again, why should these things be of importance to me? The last question for your contemplation is, if these things were not here, how would life have been?

For the most part, the bulk of humanity goes about half-asleep, or half-awake. We do not know where we are, how we got here, how the things we seek got here. Why must we seek and desire the things we crave? How much of it do we really need? Is there an order to the universe? If there is, what is our role in it? Are there things for us to give back to life, the people, and the environment?

Our compulsive ambition is grabbing as much as we can without any thought of sowing.

We only want to reap.

Karma Catches Up

But the Law of Karma inevitably catches up with us. What we run after appears to be eternally elusive. Happiness eludes us. This is Spirit's smart way of teaching us to grow up from the greedy, all-grabbing, spoiled, and ungrateful child, to become the spiritual adult who derives pleasure from appreciating all that comes their way and is always eager to give of their time, ideas, material, and spiritual possessions to make life easier for others.

When we do not appreciate the Love that Spirit has given us, we become insatiable and miserable.

Daytime Technique

Today, you will send gratitude, either in words, actions, or thoughts, to those who have loved you. Behind these people is Spirit, represented by your Guardian Angel who has been with you even before you were born.

The Secret Hand of Love

How much did you pay to your mom for bearing you for nine months in her belly? Or to your dad, who gave his sweat to make life sweet for you?

When you cried out in hunger, thirst, and discomfort, was someone not there at your beck and call to feed you and soothe your troubled brows?

In school, did you appreciate the teachers who went out of their way to groom you, though they made it tough so your future road would be smooth?

The first interview you attended, where you got that 'stupid' job, if the panel had not shown you love, would you have gotten it?

Your co-workers make going to work every morning exciting. Do you not know it is the love they give that you are tapping into?

A man walks up to you to ask you out. He is not your type, and you are pissed off, maybe a little rude to him. Have you walked through a day, a month, or a year, all well made up, looking gorgeous but no one looking in your direction, no smiles, or anyone complimenting you or asking you out?

When you are ill, you go to a clinic. Nurses and doctors fret over you, giving you their love to make sure you feel better. What if they did not exist, or you get to the clinic, and they are rude, harsh, and uncaring? What if the nurse misses the right vein while giving you the injection? What if the medicine you take for granted is not available or has never been invented?

Have you spent a whole holiday without anyone talking to you, visiting you, or calling you?

Appreciate the Love from Everywhere

Appreciate the love in your life, including the people who say hello, wave, smile, or talk to you in traffic, on the bus, or at work. It is the Love of Spirit you have too often taken for granted.

The essence of the better life you seek in this 21-day program is to have more of this Love. Appreciate it now, and you will become one with it in the future.

Notice how your day runs more smoothly when you appreciate wherever you are, and you give back to life to make this moment more enjoyable.

Love and Facebook

This appreciation of God's Love in our lives, directly and indirectly, affects our level of creativity and productivity. Let us look at talents. Talent or skill is the Love of God. Many people will ignore their talents while busy chasing after what they do not have. And they chase endlessly. Whereas someone who has a little talent but appreciates it can turn it into a wonderful enterprise.

The success story of the internet phenomenon called *Facebook* is an example. Ordinarily, the concept is almost too simple and pedestrian to warrant serious considerations by otherwise 'smart and powerful' businessmen. Platforms where people could post pictures, personal information and chat already existed before *Facebook* was created. *Yahoo Messenger*, *Hi5*, and a few others already existed. But when Mark Zuckerberg and his friends gathered to create a website to connect fellow students, a deep appreciation for what already existed and the desire to make it better ruled their hearts.

What they created was designed on the concept of love — giving and receiving it. *Facebook* has turned out to be a platform where love is appreciated; birthdays are celebrated, weddings and childbirths are welcomed with pomp and pageantry; everyday mood, actions, and hopes are posted, 'liked', 'loved', commented on, and shared. With this platform, people are being taught and encouraged to appreciate the love in life, be it in the immediate family, in the lives of colleagues, the environment, and the world. By so doing, everyone is happier, more fulfilled.

Midweek Ecstasy

Personally, this daily gratitude is like a religion for me. One of my favorite days is Wednesday which, for over two decades, I have devoted to being grateful for the love in my life. When I rise in the morning, I begin to put my attention on those who have loved me, those who have made my life worth living. There comes a rush of the most pleasant feeling into my heart and out through my heart to the world. It brings me joy and a sense of freedom. The kind of feeling you experience after you have paid all your bills and discover you have a lot of money left. Except that in this case, the joy, the peace, the sense of freedom is a deeper, ecstatic experience.

Coming right in the middle of the week, when most people are burdened with the stress of work and life in general, this midweek ecstasy is powerful and highly treasured.

Bedtime Technique

Tonight, review the day, and you will see moments where you became aware of your destiny and the role you are playing as an ambassador of God on Earth. Whatever stands out for you, please write in the journal, and enter dreamland with a heart brimming with love.

DAY TWELVE

GRATITUDE V:
LOVE YOUR BODY AND THANK GOD FOR IT

Our routine of recording our dreams should be followed strictly. By now, you should be getting used to communicating with Spirit, both when awake and when asleep. Every communication with Spirit is important.

Body like a Computer

Today, you will love your body and be grateful for it. Yes, it is like a car or a computer system, but without it, Spirit cannot experience the world. We, as Spirit, will not be able to gain access to invaluable experiences of hearing, seeing, tasting, and feeling the world where God's Love is demonstrated through good and bad, black and white, tall and short, hot and cold, pain and pleasure, birth and death. The body is a treasured vehicle.

Every Human Body Is Perfect

Every human body is perfect the way Spirit made it because everyone has a peculiar experience or mission to accomplish during our tour of duty in this world. Never compare yourself with another person, especially your body and theirs. Your body is your house of Spirit. It has its identity. Same as every other person's.

Why Were You Made as You Are?

Today, focus on every inch of your body and love it. Also, ask yourself, why did God make it the way it is?

You will get an answer from Spirit. For instance, why are you male and not female? What are the lessons and blessings that accompany that specialty? How can you use these blessings to achieve your goal of happiness?

Avoid the Worship of the Body

You do this without being carried away in an unnecessary worship of the body they call narcissism. That is worldly worship of the body, as though it's your true identity rather than Spirit. It would be an aberration if the master suddenly began to worship the servant. But the servant must be given love and be appreciated.

This is loving God by appreciating the beautiful temple It has created and put in your care, for your use, your pleasure, and pain in this short stay on Earth. Through the body, all desires, wishes, dreams, and destinies can be manifested.

Worship of the Phallus

There are many religious and philosophical beliefs in the world regarding the human body. In the ancient world, some tribes worshipped different body parts, like the phallus. That is the penis. Majority of the worshippers were women who hungered for the fruit of the womb. They believed that worshipping this body part was the solution to their problem. The rites were accompanied by colorful ceremonies and orgies that attracted virile men, young maidens, and mature women alike.

Haters of the Body

This practice was condemned by adherents of other religions that believed in a total hatred for the body and its pleasures as the way to getting God to see them as righteous and deserving of Its blessings. Another extreme position, these people subjected their bodies to mutilations and suicide to get their point across to God.

But will Spirit reward you for hating what It created? Will It also reward you for bowing to something It gave you to use as a servant?

Ironically, these two myopic positions survived the collapse of those ancient civilizations. They are still here with us. They are in religion, music, sports, movies, cultures, and traditions. Examples are our music videos, fashion shows and most of our TV adverts and shows. They, for the most part, promote the appearance of the body above character.

It Is All in the Body

In the middle is the truth, the true position: appreciate; treasure; do not hate; do not worship. Be attentive as you listen, see, and feel the Presence of Spirit moving silently and subtly, revealing to you what you desire. It is all in the body.

Bedtime Technique

In the evening, write your experiences and encounters of the day that stand out and speak to you. Go to bed with the usual practice of eagerly looking forward to exploring the Glory of God awaiting you in dreamland.

DOCTOR SPIRIT

My health was breaking down incessantly, making me a weekly visitor at the company clinic. During my daily prayer of singing the Word, my Guardian Angel had asked me to go for a walk in the sun one hour a day. I was working from 7 a.m. till 7 p.m., encased in offices lit by numerous fluorescent bulbs. These, added to the many computers I was surrounded with, made the radiation level utterly debilitating. This knowledge was not common; an office is never regarded as a house that can literally make you sick.

I began using my one-hour lunch break to take a walk in the sun. Sometimes I would walk to a restaurant about a mile from the office. Prior to this injunction, I ate in the staff canteen in the basement of the 22-story building. Invariably, between 7 a.m. and 7 p.m., I was a prisoner. But following this direction, my health improved greatly.

Vision of a Chicken

After a while, I began having repeated and severe typhoid fever. I surrendered the situation to Spirit, asking for help. Suddenly, the Spiritual Eye opened, and I saw a chicken and was told to avoid all poultry products. That was hard, but I complied. Later, when I researched online, I discovered that *Salmonella Typhi* — the bacteria responsible for typhoid fever — incubates well in dairy and poultry environment.

Giving Up Pleasures

I not only stopped eating eggs, chicken, turkey, and their by-products, but I also stopped drinking milk and eating cheese.

And just when I thought Doctor Spirit was through with me, I was asked to stop eating yam, yeast, cassava, and by-products. Now, I protested. The way we were going, soon, only water would be left on the menu for me! I stubbornly continued to eat these foods. And guess what? I got paid in a hard coin for my disobedience. A couple of times, I was hospitalized.

Imagine savoring a sweet-tasting loaf of bread with a

delicious, tongue-licking bottle of milk to wash it down, but in a few days, I had to pay thousands in money, sweat, and groans to balance my body.

Ungrateful Spoiled Brat

I realized I was being ungrateful and acting like a spoiled brat. Spirit meant well for me; that is why I was given the revelations. Why did I not mean well for myself by complying? I was being myopic. When I opened my eyes, I saw numerous cereals, fish, beef, fruits, vegetables, and nuts that go well with my body. I also discovered soymilk. And guess what? They have been here before I was born!

We All Are Work in Progress

I extended my range and scope of gratitude and began having fun all over again; healthier fun this time. I tell my friends, "When you are working with Spirit, the record is not over yet." We are all work in progress in the hands of the Master Craftsman. So, be expectant, be ready, and be on the lookout for something new from the Big Boss.

The Big Boss, you will find out, is the best friend you or anyone can ever have, especially if you learn to listen with the Inner Ear and watch carefully with the Inner Eye.

DAY THIRTEEN

GRATITUDE VI: THANK GOD FOR YOUR ENEMIES

There are no enemies. There are only teachers. Everyone has someone who makes life difficult for them. Jesus had Caiaphas. Moses had the pharaoh. Every student has a teacher who is always on their case and will give the toughest tests and exams.

That is how God made life. We all need teachers to straighten us and strengthen us. When the pot is on fire, it cries and complains; but when the food is cooked and ready to eat, the pot is like a proud mother beholding a graduating child.

Gold and the Furnace

Gold is crude and unattractive metal until burnished in the furnace. Only then is it ready for its mission in this world, which is to show humanity a glimpse of the Light of Soul that glitters when bathed in the blazing stream of Spirit.

Earth Is Not a Vacation

Why would, or should, anyone complain about people at work, in the neighborhood, on the road, and even in our family, whose actions seem to make our life difficult? Because we do not realize that coming to Earth is enrolling in the School of Hard Knocks. It is not a Bermuda Island vacation or an Obudu Cattle Ranch honeymoon.

This is not saying life is an uninterrupted hell. No, it is not. But a school is a place where we study hard, play hard, forge friendships, and have fun, but with a single, overriding goal in mind. We are there to learn lessons, be tested to see if we have learned well, and get good grades that will qualify us for service to life at a higher level. The serious students never hate their teachers. It is the lazy students' obsession to rain abuses on every member of staff, plus the classmates that appear to know it all.

Never Have Enemies

Spiritually speaking, we must never hate anyone, nor have enemies. Do not worry if some weak-minded persons choose to hate you. That is their business. It shows their level in life, spiritually. But it is your responsibility not to hate them back. Like I have said, you do not have to eat and sleep in their homes if they do not like your face. But in your heart, wish them well. Give them God's Love.

Spirit Is Testing You

When someone hates you or tries to make life difficult for you, it is a test that Spirit is giving you to see if you are deserving of the boundless Love of God that you seek. If you hate someone that God loves, why should It love you?

You Have a Weakness

Usually, a situation of strong dislike or hatred shows there is a weakness in you that the other person is reacting to. Find out what it is and correct it. It may be you have to be more discerning, and choose your friends more wisely. If you hate someone, there is something in you that you see reflected in the face, body, attitude, and beliefs of the other person. Look inward. Life is a mirror. What you see out there is what is inside you.

Daytime Technique

Today, you will fill your heart with love for Spirit, thanking It for sending the people who hate, dislike, or make life difficult for you. Only then can you enter the Ocean of God's Love where all you need for happiness exists.

Bedtime Technique

During the day, and in dreamland, you will receive messages from Spirit. Be attentive. It will be in the language you have developed and agreed with Spirit. Write these messages, nudges, intuitions, visions, spiritual Light, and Sound in your journal before you sleep.

Your journal is your personal Holy Book; be faithful to it. In no time, you will see that God, the Guardians, and Spirit care as much for you as they do the great men and women you have always admired. You will see it in these experiences you record in your journal.

DAY FOURTEEN

GRATITUDE VII: THANK GOD FOR THE GOOD IN THE LIFE OF OTHERS

Today is a Saturday — if you followed the instruction to start this adventure on a Sunday. So many people dedicate it to social get-together. Most of us do not recognize these events as spiritual. Yes, they are! Yes, people devote the day to drinking, over-eating, loud music, dancing, indulging in the vanities and pleasures of the flesh.

All those are some of the ways to share the Love of God and give gratitude for life. Yes, there are wrong ways to do a right thing. But doing nothing is worse. A thing done badly can be improved upon; it can be corrected. A thing not done at all cannot be done better or improved upon.

Celebrate Others

Most people 'celebrate' as a way of giving gratitude to God for life. That is okay. Our own focus today is to give God the glory for the goodness in others. We shall appreciate others. Everyone has the goodness of God. Can we identify these things and be grateful for them?

Recognizing Talents of My Colleagues

In school, I noticed some of my colleagues had distinct talents. Bidemi could make anyone laugh, and he became a renowned MC. Niji could direct, and he did so effortlessly. He later went on to win several international movie awards. Yemi and Segun were fantastic actors, and they became world-famous. Tunde was a critic with a keen eye for detail, picking out little omissions and additions to make a creative work much better. Taiwo was a good-hearted, jovial fellow with the gift of the garb. He went on to become the General Overseer of a church.

Many a time, I would watch these guys and marvel at the source of their talents. Because of my spiritual exposure at that time, it was easy for me to appreciate their talents; and I regularly did so after every production. I could have disliked them, envied them, or distanced myself from them.

Envy Closes the Gateway

To receive from Spirit, you must appreciate the goodness It has deposited in others. A lack of appreciation, or envy, only closes the gateway between Spirit and us.

In case you have not noticed, the next time a feeling of envy or jealousy passes through your consciousness, you will notice a choking or constricting feeling around the heart area and in the throat. Your heart races; your breathing becomes shallow. That reflects what is taking place in the aura and spiritual bodies. At that moment, you have blocked the flow of the Current coming from God or the Source. You have shrunken. If it persists, you might be setting the stage for a serious illness.

Vanity Makes You Small

A major stumbling block in the mind of man is vanity. The opposite is humility. Vanity makes you small, while humility expands your heart and vision. Vanity is the quality of exaggerated self-worth. We think we are the most important thing in the world. Yes, we are the most important thing created, but so is every other person, animal, plant, and rock. These things emanate from the Body and Heart of the Source. If some are more important and others are inferior, you are saying sometimes God is important, sometimes It is inferior.

Vanity makes us look down on our neighbors and friends. We think they are not loved by God that is why they do not have the looks we have, the mansions and cars we have. We think the Grace of God is meant for ourselves, and others must be the children of the devil.

Worshiping the Golden Calf

Phrases, such as, 'man of God', 'the chosen people', 'children of God', 'the blue bloods', 'the rich gang', are just glamorized worship of the self and personality. We are raising up the golden calf — made of glittering metals — for worship.

Even the Famous Artiste…

When we think we are greater than others, we are telling Spirit we are self-sufficient. We do not need Its Love. We can take care of ourselves. But can we? Even the famous artistes who glorify money, in sober moments thank God for Its mercies. If they look at the dollars they boast about, they would see and smell the sweat of the so-called 'common folks' who made sacrifices to buy their products. The same applies to the businessman, politician, manager, pastor, athlete, actor who thinks they are better than the next person.

Yes, you have skills the other person does not have, but if the president did not have a bodyguard, a cook, a janitor, and a nurse, he would not be president. He would be a regular bloke struggling to make ends meet like the guy down the street.

Happy People Are Happy for Happy People

Let me draw our attention to a germane but easily overlooked fact. Generally, when we speak about vanity, our minds go to the feeling of superiority over others. Yes, for the most part, it is easy to be vain if you think you are better than another person either in wealth, looks, or intelligence. But what is easily overlooked is that this feeling also applies to someone who has less, or is even poor, but thinks the other person does not deserve to be happy.

This is vanity expressed by those who are spiritually poor. It does not matter if the person is materially rich or otherwise. They are never happy to see others happy.

Happy people are always happy for others. Loving people are always happy to see others in love. A rich heart is always happy to see others get rich, either materially or spiritually.

Even when a woman is desperately searching for a baby, she MUST rejoice to see another woman give birth to her third or fourth child. If she is not, then she is not ready to receive the same from God. You must never forget that the baby you have or do not have, the riches you have or do not have, the job you have or do not have, the good health you have or do not have are given by God on whom you wait patiently.

Ignorance of this spiritual law has been the source of man's unhappiness and self-inflicted ill-health. The body, emotions, and mind of man are built to function with the ingestion of Love Energy or Current flowing from Spirit, which is the Essence of God. When we block the flow, we hasten our death, prolong our suffering and unhappiness.

The clergy and moralists take the wrong approach by

begging man to love his neighbor. They promise man a place in heaven if he does so. They threaten him with a spot in hell if he does not. But the truth is that no man should be begged to love his neighbor. Every human Soul is programmed to be a conduit pipe for love, to give and receive it. The moment an individual stops giving and receiving love, the fail-safe 'Spiritual Anti-virus System' is activated. The consequences are anxiety, sadness, ill-health, confusion, high-blood pressure, neurosis, and other debilitating conditions.

Anything inimical to love is a spiritual virus.

Appreciating the goodness in the life of others is appreciating the goodness in your life at present, or that will come to you. It is an essential spiritual technique for your physical, mental, and spiritual well-being.

Bedtime Technique

Go to bed after observing your quiet moment. Review the spiritual journey of the day. See and note those moments when you soared in Spirit by being appreciative of others. You are a step closer to the Heart of God.

Tosin King James 92

DAY FIFTEEN

MEET YOUR GUARDIAN ANGEL

There is the divine teacher, comforter, healer, and prophet whom I wish to call the 'Spirit-Son' for the purpose of this book so as not to be limited by Its different religious concepts. It is the Holy Spirit in a male form. The Spirit-Son is not a human being like you and me. It is God but sometimes takes human form. It has appeared to humanity using different human vessels. Some are known, while others were unknown but quietly served God and all life until their time was done.

Beyond Religion

When they are alive, they are beyond religion, but their followers usually set up an organization or movement after they are gone, to preserve the teachings. Invariably, as typical of material things, decay and depreciation soon catch up with the sanctity of these teachings. But the Spirit-Son is always at hand to assist all sincere Souls.

Redeemer of All Souls

The Spirit-Son, however, cannot be limited by body, matter, space, or religion. As God-personified, It has an intrinsic link to every Soul in existence. It teaches all, whether they be Muslim, Christian, ECKist, or pagan.

Some call It Christ; others address It as Allah, Krishna, or Jehovah. To others It is Mahanta, while some just say, 'my conscience', '*chi*', 'my God'. It is the redeemer of all Souls.

Saints, Servants, and Masters

On Earth, and in the Heavens, there are thousands of very advanced Souls that I call Saints or Masters who are servants of God and God alone. They work under the direction of the Spirit-Son to assist all who call on God for assistance. Some have come from China, India, Israel, Africa, America, while others came from other planets within our solar system and beyond. Most are male, but there are many ladies in their ranks. A meeting with any one of them will leave you changed forever. Happier you shall be. Wiser and freer is anyone lucky to have had this experience.

One of the jobs of these Saints is to take a willing and ready Soul into the Heavens to experience God and encounter Spirit firsthand. The trip to the Second Heaven — where the future can be viewed like a movie — is under the guidance of these Saints, who are also called Guardian Angels by those who have enjoyed the help, guidance, healing, wisdom, and protection these worthy Sons and Daughters of God give to those who open their hearts to love.

The Third Heaven, known as the Mental Plane, is a beautiful region to visit in the company of your Guardian. Here is where most of the wise men and women in the history of this planet have made their destination of choice. This is where knowledge, intelligence, concepts, advanced sciences, democracy, and other political and economic systems are brewed. It is an expansive region where the best of religion, music that uplifts, healing techniques, especially regarding mental health, astrology, numerology, medical practice, technological advancements, languages, educational templates are found and developed before being downloaded to the physical.

Most people who advocate for change, innovation, and development, especially the type that will benefit mankind as a whole, have been taken to this region and trained, either in their sleep or awake. Most leaders of thought like Rev. Martin Luther King Jr., Nelson Mandela, Albert Einstein, George Washington, Indira Gandhi, Mahatma Gandhi, Winston Churchill, Abraham Lincoln, Barack Obama, Yanni, Michael Jackson, Oprah Winfrey, Malala Yousafzai, Karl Max, Chairman Mao, Mother Teresa, Queen Elizabeth, Orville and Wilbur Wright, Bill Gates, Jeff Bezos, Enya, Mark Zuckerberg, William Shakespeare and most writers, to mention a few, have visited these regions to learn, or to be inspired, at one time or the other, some more frequently than others.

Anyone and everyone can visit these regions for the purpose of enriching their personal lives, but more importantly for the purpose of serving life. Truth is, most people do so but are unconscious of it. Your Guardian Angel — your tour guide, teacher, and healer — is ready when you are.

A Loving Heart, the Only Sacrifice

To meet with these wonderful Lights, you must be prepared. That is what you have been doing in the last fourteen days. They are not people of religion, so they ask not for the sacrifice of sheep and goats, neither do they ask for tithes. They do not use candles, oil, or ashes. The only quality they insist you have is a loving heart — a heart devoid of hate, anger, complaints, vanity, and worship of material things and persons. These character defects are obstacles or roadblocks between Spirit and us.

Spiritual Names of the Guardians

Today, being Sunday, if you go to church, mosque, or the ECK temple, you will have only one inner desire — to meet with your Guardian Angel who oversees giving you this revelation, healing, or wisdom that you seek. In some other books, I mention names of some Saints who gave me revelations for mankind. In other instances, I do not name the Saint, either because I do not know or it is unnecessary. Often, they do not tell you their names, especially if they are making a fleeting appearance. Also, some of them have been known by different names. It may be confusing or misleading to give names. Be that as it may, all of them have their spiritual names. They will reveal these as you relate more closely with them.

Daytime Technique

Today, you will invite your Guardian Angel by chanting or singing 'Guar-dian Ang-el'. You can chant or sing the name of a Guardian or Master if you are familiar with him or her. If you can take a stroll that lasts up to an hour, take your time, and chant it under your breath. As you do so, imagine him or her as a being with Light and Love radiating from their heart. This technique uses the imagination just as you use the cell phone to call a friend.

Take It Serious

If you feel more comfortable with Rama, Jesus, Saint Francis of Assisi, or a Muslim Saint you know, like Rumi, Kabir, or Shamus, feel free to imagine them and invite their presence by chanting their name. Be aware, this is no child's play. These agents of God are extremely pure-hearted beings and extremely busy. If you call on the president of your country, you better be serious. And the Saints are not in the same rank as your president.

As you walk down the road, imagine this Saint approaching you with a smile. Light shines from their heart to your heart. Hear them call you by name. See their hair, clothes, up to their feet. Do not ask for anything. Just send love to them.

If you cannot take a walk, then sit in a chair, or lie in bed, and take the walk in your imagination, down a wooded trail, or on a beach with palm trees and cool breeze coming from the ocean. Then, see the Guardian walk up to you. Use whatever works for you as a serene and peaceful environment. Even if it is a library or soccer stadium filled with thousands of shouting fans. We are all wonderfully but differently made.

It Works Wonders

For those who are more sensitive to the spiritual worlds, especially women, this technique works wonders. You may see him or her as imagined. You may see someone else who is totally different from what you imagined. You may see the Light or hear the Sounds of Spirit. You may suddenly find yourself fully awake in one of the Heavens. You may be taken to the future. Some may just have an understanding or insight. Whatever it is, write it in your journal and contemplate on it.

ANNA'S HEAVENLY ENCOUNTER

Anna was born a Catholic and a devoted one she grew up to be. She knew about Saints and Guardian Angels, but she had never met any. A thing of faith and belief it was for her.

We used to talk about divine helpers. They are God's

people, not limited by faith or philosophy, but once you open your heart to God, to love, they will come to you.

"More Real than a Dream"

One morning, Anna called to say she had had a remarkable dream that "looked more real than a dream." This is a conscious journey to the Heavens while asleep. This is not a collection of jumbled scenes we call a dream. It is as real as being awake.

She had been at what looked like a school with many classrooms. She felt at home since I was there too. To her observation, the class members all looked younger and fresher, with glowing skin. This is the nature of the First Heaven. But what struck her the most was a slim, tall, grey-haired, and bearded man who looked at her with the most loving and powerful eyes she had ever seen. "It's like he's divine," Anna gushed.

Saint of the Book of Revelations

She is lucky to have been invited to one of the temples in the heavenly worlds, where the Saint who gave John the *Book of Revelation* teaches the ways of Spirit to those who open their arms, ready for the Holy Embrace. Anna was never the same again.

From her account of what transpired in this vivid journey into the heavenly world, no word was ever spoken between her and this Saint. All he did was to stare directly at her without uttering a word. But what he was giving her was the Blessing of the Ancient One. This is the Power of Spirit channeled through the Saint to the lucky Soul.

Physical Appearance of Guardian Saints

Some have reported having physical encounters with a Guardian Saint who appears physically but posing as either a beggar or a casual passerby or wayfarer. In these cases, the persons they are visiting do not recognize them. And, of course, they will not come to you and say, "Hi, I'm a Guardian Angel, and I've come with a blessing." That would probably freak you out, and you would take off or call the police to have the 'cranky' fellow arrested. However, if you believe it is an Angel, you would probably be too excited, too emotionally convoluted to be receptive to whatever they have come to give you. Invariably, the best option is what the Saints adopt when making a physical appearance — they disguise. Unless you have the spiritual stamina to remain detached in their presence.

Bedtime Technique

At day's end, review the day's walk and experiences in your mind; then, invite your Guardian Angel into your dreams. He or she will be waiting on you as you leave the clay shell temporarily to enter a more expansive world, though for a short while.

DAY SIXTEEN

CONVERSE WITH YOUR GUARDIAN ANGEL

It is Monday. You wake into another week of hustle and bustle, but your life has changed. You are no longer the angry and fearful person. Now you know you are surrounded by friends like Spirit, the Spirit-Son, and your Guardian Angel. Yesterday, you took a walk and met with your Guardian. In the night, you spent time with them in dreamland. This morning, you entered the encounter in your journal.

Very Important Holy Person

Monday is our day of gratitude for our possessions, both tangible and intangible, the ones we can see and the ones that cannot be held. One more thing you now possess is your intimate friendship with a Very Important Holy Person (VIHP). If you knew the president, your physical life would transform; but knowing a VIHP transforms both your physical and spiritual life. Now you are being inducted into the Elite Club of Spirit.

HU-Mana

Today, you will sing a sacred Word: HU-Mana. Two sacred Words joined together to serve as a vehicle to take us into the future. It will also heal us of past hurts of the mental and emotional kinds. Our ability to properly align with our destiny on Earth will be enhanced as we sing these words.

HU, the Word of Creation

The word HU is the Word of Creation with which everything came into existence. It is not anyone's language, neither is it a symbol. Rather, it is the Power of Spirit that brings all Creation to manifest. In the biblical Pentecostal experience, it was heard as the rushing, mighty wind. That is how it sounds when the Power and Spirit of God, flowing from Its Heart, or the Throne of Grace, contacts the Spirit of man. Light, or fire, accompanies this encounter like the 'tongue of fire' of Pentecost and 'the burning bush' of Moses. When you hear this Voice or Music of God, your heart is cleansed, freed, and lifted into Its Presence.

Mana, Power of the Second Heaven

The second Word, 'Mana', is the Power of God coming into the Second Heaven where the memory of the past and future is stored. This is also where the seeds of all that can be are stored in a latent format waiting to be 'downloaded' by man. Mana activates the mind and memory of man. From this Word was crafted the word, 'man'. The word, 'Human' is HU and Mana, which, invariably, means the Spirit of God dwelling in flesh and mind. The human being is an intricate mix of the Spirit of God, mind, and flesh. This is one of the sacred secrets of our existence that are hidden in plain sight. And because of its simplicity, those who seek meaning in complicated and expensive terrains will miss it.

Entrance Into the Chamber of Prophecy

To activate our true spiritual potential and identity, we should sing HU regularly. To gain entrance into the Chamber of Prophecy or to craft a new life, a new image, a new reality, we should sing HU-Mana or Mana. In case you are skeptical of words, the origin of which you do not know, then sing HU-man. You can see *The Book of Prophecies* for more on the secrets of the sacred Words and the modern miracles being wrought *through* those who sing them with a heart of love.

Converse with Your Guardian

As you go through the day, sing HU-Mana. Have a conversation with your Guardian Angel on your life and the future you would like to know, or the new reality you would like to 'download' into your life. Be grateful for their presence. Even if you have not seen them, they are with you, and they hear the thoughts and feelings that emanate from you.

TINA, THE THOMAS

Sometime in 2014, I met Tina (not her real name). She was a natural skeptic about the authenticity of sacred Words.

"I don't believe in it," she said, rather bluntly. "If I don't believe in it, then it can't work for me," she rationalized.

After thirty years of singing sacred Words, I knew she was wrong. We are not talking about the imagination or faith. The Word HU is the Name of God, the Creative Fiat that the Source issued at the moment of initial Creation. Anywhere it is uttered, God's Presence fills that space and time. Whoever sings or chants it will feel this sacred Presence. Even when you just listen to it being sung, or a recording of it, you will feel God's Presence.

Though Tina was skeptical, she still wanted to know more. "I can give you a demonstration. I will sing it for five minutes. You can just listen, with your eyes open or shut."

"What Really Is This HU?"

She agreed. I closed my eyes while she sat beside me, holding on to her skepticism. After a few minutes, she shut her eyes but did not sing along.

When I was done, she looked at me and asked, "What really is this HU?"

Wind from Heaven

"It's the Name of God, as I said. It is the Wind from Heaven, mighty and rushing. It brings with it the full force of the Presence of Spirit."

She was silent for a while; then she said, "I didn't even sing it, but I saw things."

"That's nice. Things like what?"

Tina Sees the Future

"I was on the road. There was a bike. I said something to the rider, but I can't remember. It was so vivid."

"That's quite nice. You were in the Spirit, and probably shown a future event."

She waved it off; soon, other issues overtook our attention. About half an hour later, I saw her off to get a taxi. But she saw a commercial bike and said she preferred it to a taxi. Stopping the bike, I watched and listened closely. She began an unusual conversation with the bike man, asking if he knew a particular direction different from his normal route. Then she brought out some money from her purse. Next, she was asking him for change.

"Does this look or sound familiar? Your spiritual experience with the bike man?"

She thought for a second and nodded. "Somehow,"

she answered cautiously.

Tina had been given a prophetic experience that was in the future, about an hour away. Her skepticism did not wear off just because of this. She still did not believe in the power of the Word. But Spirit was not done with her.

The Name Sets You Free

Before we met, she was a regular at the monthly deliverance service held in her church. She was regular because after deliverance, the demons would leave her for a while then return with renewed force. The attacks always left her fearful of going to bed or sleeping at night. Her nights were sleepless; she stayed up playing worship songs and praying for hours. This left her tired and sleepy during the day.

"If you call the true Name of God, you'll be set free."

"I don't believe in it, so it can't work for me," she repeated stubbornly.

Encounter in Dreamland

After that, I never spoke about it again, until one morning when she called my cell phone at 4.30 a.m.

She said she had just had a remarkable spiritual encounter in dreamland. As usual, the demonic powers had surrounded and chained her, ready for the kill. She shouted and chanted the holy words she knew. But it was all in vain.

When she was about to lose the battle, she became aware of a sacred presence. It was one of the Guardian Angels I am very familiar with: a tall, slim man with a full head of snow-white hair and long, white beard. His skin is the color of Middle Eastern people. Usually, he does not say much, but his eyes issue power that sets free anyone who stares into them.

"Sing HU!" He commanded in a soft but firm voice.

She would have protested, but here she was, after chanting all the names and tongues she knew and believed in, yet the demons were about snuffing life out of her.

Tina Is Delivered

Tina, left with no choice, sang the sacred Word. What followed was miraculous. The demonic men and women were first startled before catching fire and exploding into oblivion. She was shocked that something she did not believe in could work, and in such a miraculous way too.

This encounter did not make Tina develop a waking life belief in the Word, but she never stopped singing it in the Spirit world. We may look at Tina as unnecessarily skeptical, but most of us would not readily give up our old ways for new ones, no matter how life-changing. Tina's trepidation stemmed from attachment to her comfort zone. But when the familiar zone is no longer comfortable, we should be wise enough to give up our loyalty to what has stopped working.

HU Man

"Hi HU-man!" she always hailed whenever she talked to me on the phone or bumped into me.

"That's me," I would reply. "Anytime you say HU-man, you're affirming the God-ness in yourself and in others."

The Saints and Guardian Angels are at hand to offer a helping hand, but we must make an effort. They have absolute respect for our right to express our will. They will not intrude unless we call to God for help after exhausting our arsenal of pride and power.

Bedtime Technique

At night, sit in a chair or lie on your back and sing any of the sacred Words. Fifteen minutes should be enough. Afterward, remain silent while you watch the Spiritual Eye and listen to the Inner Sound. Continue the conversation with your Guardian. More importantly, listen to them. They will have a message, a gift, a blessing for you.

Then, sleep.

DAY SEVENTEEN

LAND OF THE ORANGE SUN

Today, wake up feeling grateful to God for Its Presence in your life through your Guardian Angel who has been with you before you knew they existed. You will continue the conversation with them throughout the day.

First, review your dreams of the night. You must have met with him or her in the dream world. Do you remember? Then write down the encounter. What did they say to you? Or, you only remember seeing your friend, or dad, or a loved one telling you something important? Please, write it down. Probably, it has to do with your health, education, career, or love life, as you have desired to know? Or is it something completely different? Spirit uses symbols and images, even the form of someone close to us, to pass across a message. And, sometimes, the message we get is completely far afield from our range of thoughts and mind. The reason is that God and your Guardian Angel know you much better than you know yourself.

So, you think getting a man to love you or buying a house will make your life happier? Rather, you get a revelation telling you to go apply for a diploma you do not appear to need. You may want to discountenance it, but Spirit sees everything and knows everything. Maybe while studying for the diploma that is when and where you will meet your sweetheart. Maybe from there you will travel and will not need a new house.

Listen and Obey

You would never know what Spirit has in store for you if you do not listen to and obey the messages from Spirit. Writing these encounters is the beginning of wisdom. Whatever the personality, the drama, or the messages in your dreams, value them and meditate on them when you wake.

During the day, continue to quietly sing HU-Mana, Guard-ian Ang-el, Ma-na, or simply HU, as you may find convenient. Then place your attention lightly on the ongoing conversation with your Angel. Let this be as natural and unobtrusive as possible.

Beyond Prophets and Therapists

By now, if you have had the desired revelation, you can move on to another aspect of your life that you desire to know or ask for more information on the initial issue. Once you have opened the line of communication, do not close it. We all need Spirit's Wisdom in every area of our lives. An everyday awareness of your Guardian Angel is a huge boost. And what can be better? They do not charge per hour like human prophets and therapists!

Continue with the Disciplines

All you need is to continue the disciplines we have discussed since **Day One**. You must continually clean up your temples and continually do the daily gratitude. You must also look at and listen to the sights and sounds of life with the wonder and eagerness of a child or a tourist. Now, in addition, you will sing the sacred Words at your convenience. Let it become second nature, an integral part of you.

Just as in your dreams, Spirit will, many a time, speak to you through others and even through nature. Be attentive and write these in your journal at day's end.

Visit the Second Heaven

Tonight, you will visit the Second Heaven with your Guardian Angel. During the day, make this request as you talk to them. Also, visualize or imagine a beautiful land where the sun is orange and the vegetation has a predominantly orange hue — a world of beautiful temples and imposing mansions made of precious stones, the same as the highways. Everyone is radiant, ageless; they appear to live forever. Mind you, there are higher Heavens filled with greater wonders.

Also, note that wherever you are, these Heavens are with you. Even if you do not see them, the consciousness that pervades these lofty and sacred places can be with you. Thus, the saying, "My heart is in heaven, while my feet are firmly planted on Earth."

They Glow

It is easy to know those who have entered these Glories. They glow with an invisible Light. They are happy, gracious, grateful, and graceful people. Above all, they treat all of life with kindness, love, and respect. The purpose of a spiritual life is for us to be the best human being God created. It is not to take from life, from Guardian Angels, and the Heavens without sowing into life seeds of love, seeds of charity, seeds of compassion, seeds of wisdom that help to make life easier for the next person. Life is not a one-way traffic.

How to Love God

The only way to love God is to love your neighbor as yourself. At a stage, we reach the level of the Saints and

Guardian Angels who love us more than we love our vanities. They spend every moment in service to Spirit by helping us. Their joy comes from seeing us grow, not unlike a sweet mother who starves herself so that her baby might have the little food available.

GLORIA'S MARITAL WOES

Gloria grew up as a brilliant, vibrant lady, exceptionally dexterous at whatever she took an interest in. Early in life, as a hyperactive extrovert, she immersed herself in academics, sports, and business. Many opportunities came her way. She acquired the material valuables of life while still a teenager. She traveled the world and became the toast of many upwardly mobile, dashing young men.

It was not a surprise to many of her friends that, while they were still writing college exams, Gloria was getting married. A few were happy for her. But secretly, many were envious, and a few were resentful. Was she the only one the world was made for? Her seniors in the family were still praying for men to look their way, but Gloria was already controlling the most handsome and most powerful of them all. Because of this secret resentment, only a handful of young ladies ever ventured to keep her company or be her friend. She ended up with a larger number of male friends.

Gloria was not particularly imbued with a superiority complex. In fact, she was oblivious to the jealousy and envy. Her main preoccupation was to focus on her business and family. Her husband doted on her because he loved the admixture of a goal-getter career lady and a devoting wife and mother. She was his dream come true.

But one year, just before she turned 25, her world

came crashing down like a castle built in the sand. The relationship with her husband turned sour; her business and career began crumbling right in her palms. Her peace of mind took a leave of her, and her erstwhile soaring fortunes appeared to have nose-dived like a craft destined for a crash.

This series of setbacks continued unabated until she was pushed to making the rounds of religious and mystical circles in the city. Her mom was helpful, introducing her to prophets and occultists she knew. But there was no reversal of her condition until she met someone familiar with other ways of contacting Spirit. She was given the sacred Word to sing, to surrender her case to Spirit for help. She enthusiastically practiced the spiritual technique. After thirty minutes, she slept, only to wake up in the Spirit body confronted by a huge Guardian Saint of chocolate skin color who asked if she was ready to know the source of her woes, to which she promptly said, yes.

The Saint opened a door behind which Gloria's mom emerged in a demonic form. She promptly made to pounce on her child. But the Guardian Angel protected Gloria and banished the demon.

Gloria woke from what she considered a nightmare, her heart racing wildly. She could not believe what she had just experienced. Her first understanding of the dream was as a metaphor. She thought it must be a metaphor Spirit had contrived to give her a message. The monster in her dream could not be her real mom, she thought to herself. Yes, that could be true but not in this case.

To clear up the doubts, she went to pay her mom a visit the following day. All her doubts vanished when she got to her mom's place. The older woman, on setting eyes on Gloria, hissed out of disdain. She was openly hostile and would not sit down to chat with her daughter.

"I have some important business to attend to. You have to leave. I will call you when I want to see you." She picked up her car keys and headed out. Gloria had no choice but to leave.

It is an understatement to say Gloria was shaken to her spiritual marrow. How do you handle a situation in which your closest friend, who has been 'helping' you through the hard times, taking you to pastors, imams, and *babalawos* for deliverance, was the architect of the whole trauma?

Lesson to Learn

How did she handle it? Most of us would not handle it well, but she applied discipline and tact. She had been told by the Saints that she had a lesson to learn from being attacked by an otherwise loving mother to whom she confided her innermost heart. It was a turbulent time for her and her mom.

She began the healing process by refraining from revealing her secrets, dreams, and troubles to mommy. She also stopped the habit of following her everywhere for 'spiritual consultation'. She sang the Word day and night, sometimes for an hour at a stretch. She received the Grace of God, and her peace of heart returned with her finances.

No One Is an Enemy; Everyone Is a Teacher

Her spiritual stature also improved. She began to learn detachment and forgiving her enemies. She learned that no one is an enemy; rather, everyone is her teacher. The encounter also taught her to quit depending on human love but only on the Divine, who has the key to true Love. Only Spirit has the power to bring us men and women who can love us genuinely.

Bedtime Technique

Before you sleep, sit in your prayer chair, and send love and gratitude to your Guardian Saint. Ask to be taken on a trip to the Land of the Orange Sun. Sing HU-Mana for ten to fifteen minutes, and sleep.

DAY EIGHTEEN

VISIT TOMORROW

How was your journey to the Second Heaven last night? You must have a huge smile on your face and a radiance that friends and colleagues will notice. Even if you do not remember the details of the trip, nonetheless, your Guardian Angel must have taken you to one of the places in that vast universe.

A Dream in a Dream

Let us look at some details of your dreams. Did you see the wonderful sights of that world? If not, do you remember the feeling of being on a mountain top and diving? Or from a plane skydiving? Or you woke up in your dream to discover you had been dreaming, at the same time you were aware of being asleep on Earth in your room? That means you went to the Second Heaven where you had some experiences and then woke up in the First Heaven before waking up here on Earth.

A dream in a dream is an indication of a trip to the higher Heavens, sometimes beyond the Third Heaven.

How about the stranger that was with you, showing you around? There is something familiar about him or her, but you cannot remember that face on Earth? Most likely, that was your Guardian Angel.

Did you say, "But s/he had no wings?"

The Saints I am talking about do not have wings. They are like you and me as far as physique is concerned. They might be surrounded by Light, but, generally, they look simple and sometimes ordinary. However, they are far above the angels with wings.

You are making progress, but you must keep the disciplines of gratitude, cleaning up the temples, singing the sacred Words, and opening the eyes and ears. This helps to open the Inner Ear and Inner Eye.

Clothes and Colors of Tomorrow

Today, the conversation with your new best friend continues. The focus is on how to improve your life. Let us add some fun to the day. You will see tomorrow. Pick something like, "What's the color of the shirt Richie will be wearing tomorrow?" Then ask your Guardian Angel the question. Listen and look for the answer. It will come.

You might hear their voice, or an impression, or the innocent bystanders gossiping about dresses and colors. It might be on a billboard or in a newspaper. Look out for it. Write the answer down in your journal and watch out for Richie tomorrow. Now, you cannot wait for tomorrow. That is part of the fun!

Bedtime Technique

At day's end, when you sing the Word and talk with your Angel, further ask to be shown a scene or event that will be happening tomorrow.

SUNDAY OR TUESDAY?

Several years ago, just after finishing school, I did a casual supervisory work on a project. It was a week's job, and all the workers were to be paid at the end of the week. We met with the manager, who informed us that he had to travel to the company headquarters in Lagos to bring our paychecks.

We were meeting with him on Friday. He was already set on his way to board a bus that would take him to Lagos.

"When are you coming back?" one of my colleagues asked.

"I would have said tomorrow, but I need to make allowance for an extra day in case I don't finish early tomorrow. The checks are ready. I just have to put in some documents to back up the approval."

I noticed he had not mentioned the day he was returning, so I asked him directly. "When are you coming back and when shall we come for our checks?"

When he spoke, the prophetic message came out in an interesting manner. He said one thing, but Spirit superimposed another, which was the truthful future.

"Definitely, *Insha* Allah, I'll be back Sunday, latest. By Monday, you guys will be smiling all the way to the bank."

My colleagues smiled and thanked him. Sunday was just around the corner. But Spirit had said "Tuesday" very loud and clear. Not physically, but my Spiritual Ear had picked it up.

Tuesday was not good. We were all broke. There was no way my guys would have smiled if the manager had said Tuesday. But that was what I had heard. So, what did I do? I asked my colleagues if the man had said Tuesday or Sunday. One or two of them looked at me with a puzzled expression.

"The man said Sunday," Clem answered, patiently.

"That's why he said we'll be going to the bank on Monday," he added, as if explaining to a five-year-old.

"Sorry, I didn't hear him right. I thought he said Tuesday."

"Too much cassava is not good for the medulla oblongata," Clem shot back with a smile.

"Nice one, Clem. I can't wait to return the compliment," I replied jokingly.

As it turned out, the manager did not show up Sunday evening. By Monday, we were at his office first thing in the morning. I knew he was not going to be there, but I had to play along. He eventually came back to town on Tuesday afternoon. Before we could go to the bank, it was Thursday. By then, no one was smiling except my humble self, marveling at how Spirit knows everything and reveals it to those who are open and ready to receive the blessings.

SAVED FROM AUTO CRASH

I was on a three-hour trip. It was a Friday, and I was giving gratitude to God for those who make life difficult. In addition, I was 'walking' in Spirit from that moment to the end of the journey.

Walking-in-Spirit Technique

This is a spiritual technique that almost everyone uses moment by moment, albeit unconsciously. When we want to embark on a mission, project, or a journey, we instinctively 'walk in the Spirit' (or in the imagination). We move from the starting point, through the space between where we are to our desired destination or goal. It is a simple technique that employs the imagination, the Spiritual Eye, the Spiritual Ear, the mind, and emotions.

If done with the right knowingness, it is a gateway to the future. This was what I was doing, but with a few other techniques accompanying it to give me the desired result.

Suddenly, I was taken to about fifteen minutes in the future. In that future, it was raining heavily, and the highway was slippery. A truck bearing a full load of crates of beer overtook our 18-seater bus. In the process, our driver lost control and crashed into the truck. The resultant scene was a sea of blood.

I opened my eyes. The sky was sunny and clear, and there was no sign of any truck in the vicinity. But I knew I had been shown the destiny of this bus. I also knew Spirit had shown me as a gift. So, I returned it to Spirit. In the imagination I continued the Walking-in-Spirit technique with which I rearranged the sequence of events so as to produce a more agreeable ending. In addition, I kept singing the Word in gratitude, surrendering to the Will of Spirit.

After about ten minutes, we got to an area where it had been raining for a while. The road was wet and slippery. Soon enough, the beer-laden truck caught up with us. I knew this was the moment.

Our driver, for whatever reason, began to race with the truck, competing for the right of space. I knew what was to happen next. But I surrendered all to Spirit. Acting on an inner nudge, I looked at the driver and spoke from the Realm of Spirit. "Let him go. We don't have the same destiny."

Like pouring cold water on burning coal, our driver's aggression died instantaneously.

We did not encounter the truck again. God's Love is given when we give our love to all life.

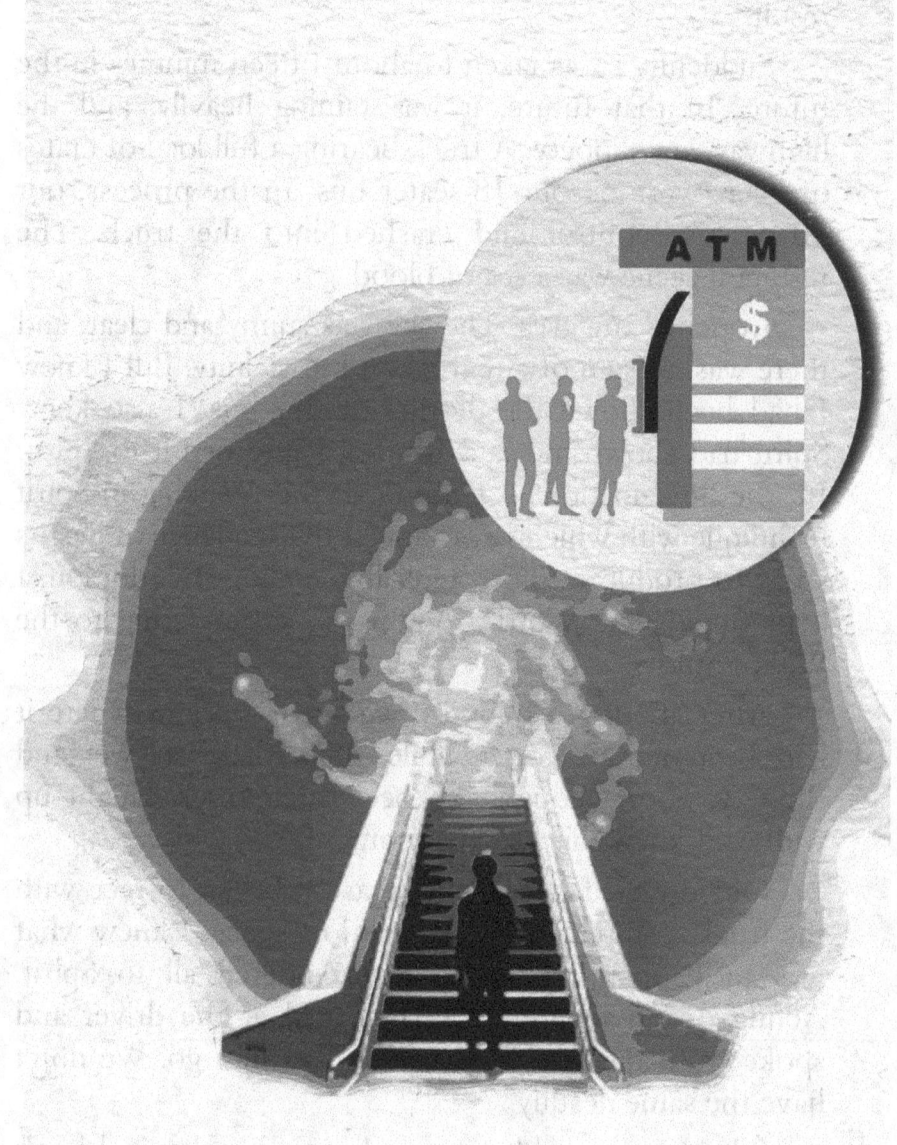

DAY NINETEEN

ANOTHER VISIT TO TOMORROW

By now, your spiritual status must have changed. Whatever your religion, if you have kept the practices in the last nineteen days you could not be the same again. Maybe you do not notice it, but your friends will. Often the last person to see the Light we radiate is ourselves. Naturally, the Light-bearer only feels the Current passing through them.

Let us look at yesterday's assignment of seeing into today. Today was tomorrow, yesterday. Now, it is just another today. Now, it feels and looks like it has always been here. This is because everything exists in the same space. The difference is the time which is relative in a very fluid manner. Time is just the sequence of movement of the events or objects in relation to one another.

Time and the ATM

In other words, the past, the present, and the future are like three people on a queue. All want to carry out the same action. For instance, at the ATM, the three want to withdraw money or use the automatic teller machine for some other purpose. All of them are in the same space, but they will insert their cards into the machine at different times. As far as the system is concerned, the other persons do not exist while one person is using it.

Secret of Prophecy and Transformation

The secret of prophecy, seeing and knowing the future, gaining the wisdom to resolve a current challenge, is to key into the Eye of Spirit, which is like the closed-circuit camera hanging atop the ATM, facing those on the queue. The camera sees everyone and everything, but the machine is aware of only the person who has inserted his card. The techniques in this book are meant to help us key into the global positioning system of Spirit.

Today, continue to look forward to seeing if the revelations you were given yesterday were correct. Do not be afraid to be wrong. It is a learning process. Next time, you will listen and see more clearly. It is also possible you got the correct answer but doubted.

Today's Assignment

Today, you may ask another question or repeat the one you began with. It may still be about Richie's dressing tomorrow. This time, when you listen, be attentive. Spirit may think you do not need to know the color of Richie's dress. There might be something more important and urgent for you to know. Any quiet moment will be used by your Angel to push an important message through. But because human beings are very busy talking or listening to junk, you might think the answers you are getting are not related to your question or desire. Do not be discouraged. If your heart is pure, and your desire will not hurt or harm another person, Spirit will surely talk to you.

SEARCHING FOR THE HOUSE AND A SONG

I was searching for a comfortable apartment in a quiet location that could afford me the opportunity to contemplate, converse with the Saints, and write these books for humanity. Physically, I had been to many house agents and checked out many vacancies. When it was getting daunting, I did the practice of asking the Guardian Saint to take me to the right house.

As I slept, I found myself in a wooded, serene, and airy environment. I was standing on the balcony, looking out at the nearby buildings. I could see the cream color of the walls quite vividly. Immediately I awoke, I began looking around for the house, but I never saw any close to it. Because of the urgency, I had to share a three-bedroom apartment.

The day we were to pay for the place, I almost blurted out that it would be temporary until the cream-colored, two-story building was ready. But I quickly reminded myself of the Law of Silence.

A few months later, there was the need to seek the quiet and peace of mind needed for creativity. I had tried to assert the right amount of effort needed to create, but I was not getting any results. Some will say I had lost my muse. But I knew I was not yet in the right house and environment that would activate the creative spirit. So, I spoke to the Guardians, and I asked them when the house that they had shown me a few months earlier would materialize.

I sat down to do another spiritual technique of seeing into the future. As I sat in quiet, a Guardian told me that they were working on it and it would be available that same week. I thanked him and went to bed. As I slept, I came awake, fully conscious in Spirit. I found myself in the same environment as the cream-colored house. However, this time I was standing on the balcony of the next house. It was raining heavily, and a particular song that I loved so much was playing while I was singing along. I looked out and saw that the house next door was my place, the cream-colored two-story building.

When I woke up in the middle of the night, I quickly wrote the encounter in my journal. Then, I spent the next thirty minutes contemplating on the details. I discovered that I was a guest of a neighbor in the house I had visited in the experience, though I could not see the neighbor's face. This could have helped me go straight to the person to ask about a vacancy in their neighborhood. But Spirit sometimes withholds vital details so that we can walk through life with some expectancy and humility.

In the morning, I did my regular prayers and surrendered the day to Spirit. While I was at it, I saw, in a flash, a picture of a place in town and Leo, a friend of mine. The silent info that came with it was that I should be at that place that day and that I would see the gentleman in question. I went to work, forgetting the whole experience.

At noon I had a strong nudge to call Leo. I asked what he would be doing after work. He replied that he was going to be at the place I had seen in the vision. I told him that we would meet there.

When we met, I mentioned my urgent need for a new place. I asked him to help look around. From the pictures I was shown, I knew he was part of the chain that would lead me to the house, though I did not know what role he was going to play. But I was pleasantly surprised when he promptly said he knew of a vacancy that met some of my requirements, especially the aspect of serenity and clean, fresh air.

"Is it a two-story building?"

"Yes," he said. "It's a duplex, actually. You can check

it out tomorrow."

"Nice. Is it yellow or cream?"

"Yes," he replied. "Why did you ask?"

I did not have to check out the house. "I'll take it," was my prompt answer. Within a week, I had moved in. I did the gratitude technique for the blessings that Spirit and the Guardians had bestowed on me by leading me to where I could do my writing.

And the Song…

About six months later, I was searching for the song I was singing in the other spiritual encounter. I did not know the title or the name of the singer. Still, I sent messages to my friends who were music experts. I tried in vain to sing the part I could remember. None of them knew the title or singer, probably because my rendition of the shred I knew must have been lousily off-key.

After searching in vain, I went back in contemplation to the inner experience of the previous year. It occurred to me that if I was singing the song in the neighbor's house, he might as well have had a copy. So, I gave him a call. Would he know where I could get the song? Yes, he did! He even had it on his playlist.

Bedtime Technique

At day's end, do the same routine as you did yesterday. Then enjoy your sleep and journey into the Heavens with your Angel.

DAY TWENTY

PLACE YOURSELF IN YOUR FUTURE

Throughout this 21-day intimate encounter with Spirit and the Angels, never tire to keep the regular disciplines. Even the simple process of writing your spiritual encounters has power on its own. In case you are physically challenged, you can make these recordings on your phone, either by writing or using the voice recorder. Every phone has one.

An important point is to keep these encounters to yourself. They are not like newspapers meant for free display at newsstands. They are more private and more intimate than what you do in the bathroom.

The prayers of singing sacred Words, as already described, are essential because these are keys for unlocking the gates of Heaven within you.

Friday for the Teachers

Today would be a Friday if you began this spiritual journey on a Sunday. As you are now aware, we dedicate today to thanking God for our teachers, those who make life difficult for us. This helps us to release one of the bonds tying us to the tempter. His mission is to make us forfeit our spiritual heritage, which exists in the Bosom of Spirit. How can we get to God when we hate and do battle with God's children? Then, we hate God. We hate our neighbors; we hate God. We love our neighbors, we love God. Knowing this simple spiritual secret, the tempter brings up disaffection, anger, and hatred between us and others.

Of course, we cannot always agree with everyone. In fact, there are some people we must never agree with because they will lure or drag us into spiritual quagmire. But that does not make us hate them. They are just a source of temptation or test to know if we have overcome the same weaknesses they exhibit. Let us appreciate our enemies and haters, for they are our mirror.

Daytime Technique

Today, we continue our conversation with our Guardian Angel. We can sing their name if we are lucky to have been told during our recent journeys into the Heavens together. If not, you can just sing the familiar sacred Words. Rather than seeing into the details of the following day, you will place yourself, or try to be aware, or imagine you are already at that moment in the future, the state of health, or the condition of living that you desire, and you are living it in the present. Do this in your mind only; assume you are there.

This is just like a daydream or what we do every time we are traveling to a place or going to work. In our mind, we imagine we are there already and try to see and feel what we will meet or experience when we arrive. It is a powerful but simple technique we all use to see the future. Whether we are conscious of the process or take note of what we are seeing and hearing in that future is a matter of the level of our spiritual maturity.

Like a Child

Use this art of seeing, hearing, and feeling to become one with that future. Discuss with your Guardian Angel within the imagination. Note the impressions you get. If done with love and expectation and excitement, like we do when on vacation or on a fun ride, you will get a good response from the Guardian Angel and Spirit. This is what Jesus meant when he said, "Unless you become like a child, you will not enter the Kingdom." The adult relies on the mind, which is just like a computer (garbage in, garbage out), whereas the child relies on the imagination, which feeds on Spirit.

The mind is a very useful and powerful tool. But it has also become the bane of our happiness, peace of mind, good health, and spiritual freedom. How come something so useful is also a source of our problems? Here is why: The mind is built to operate within set parameters, laws, restrictions, set data, set boundaries, like computers. It only knows what it is given. It may project possibilities based on the data it has been fed. But it cannot exceed the possibilities presented by the data.

Conversely, the imagination is designed to exceed boundaries set by the senses. It feeds on higher impulses given by Spirit. It is the key to a greater life.

Bedtime Technique

At day's end, record whatever impressions came to you. To assist you in remembering details, use the Rewind technique, moving from this moment that you are in bed, through the numerous events of the day, back to when you woke up in the morning.

Record whatever you heard and saw that throws more light on your future. Sit or lie down to sing HU or HU-Mana. Once again, request to be taken to the Chamber of Prophecy in the Second Heaven. Imagine taking the trip with your Guardian Angel, surrounded by uplifting orange light. Then sleep.

ALICE SEES HER FUTURE FAMILY

Alice was in a turbulent relationship with Jake. Their love was like traffic lights — constantly changing in color and never stable for too long. Today, they are passionately entwined, with kisses and roses. The next day, they are throwing brickbats at each other, cursing the day they met. The day that followed would end with apologies and lovemaking. This making-up would end with Alice asking him to marry her. But Jake would be aloof, and the cycle of 'love me or leave me alone' would enter a higher gear.

When Alice discussed the relationship with me, she was deciding to trap Jake by getting pregnant without his knowledge. She was going to wait until the pregnancy was mature enough, giving Jake no room for excuses and leaving him with few choices.

"That is the trick a smart girl can use to get her man to commit, whether he likes it or not. Nowadays, most of these dashing young men don't want to settle down in a hurry. There are too many fine babes begging for their attention."

"Why don't you talk with Spirit on this issue?" I asked her.

"What has my love life got to do with Spirit? I don't take my religion to that fanatic level. James, I love my man even though we fight occasionally. But everyone fights. My mom and dad used to fight, but they're still together after thirty years."

I looked at her with compassion. She had good arguments and logic. But no one should plan their life and happiness on logic and good arguments alone. It is always easy to win arguments, but you cannot win happiness. That comes with Grace.

I showed her how to pray with the Word and surrender to Spirit. She was excited about the possibilities of meeting wise men and women who serve as Guardian Angels.

"That won't be a bad idea," she enthused. "There are many issues I want to discuss with them."

Unknown to her, even as we discussed the issue, her Guardian Angel was standing by, waiting for an invitation. It took only five minutes of singing the Word before she met with him and went on a conscious trip into the Heavens. Very much like Paul described his journey to the Third Heaven in his Second Letter to the Corinthians, chapter 12. She was taken out of the body, and together they explored the Glories in the higher universes.

After being taken to some sacred places, where she was bathed (baptized) by the Light and Music of Spirit, he took her into the Chamber of Prophecy in the Second Heaven. To her senses, she was at a school playground where children were having fun on the swings.

Her Guardian Angel pointed her attention to a boy and a girl. "Do you recognize those two?"

"No, I don't. Who are they?"

"Those are your first two children."

She shook her head in disbelief. The boy was about seven, while the girl was about five. "How can they be my kids? I don't even have a man to marry. Jake is still playing hard to get."

The ever-wise Guardian Saint smiled and said, "Come."

Instantly, they were in a church, and it was a wedding occasion. She noticed the bride and groom exchanging their vows. When she looked closely, she saw the bride was herself. But who could her husband be? She was expecting it to be Jake, but it was not.

This was a shock to her senses. Why would she be getting married to a stranger and not the man who turned her head? The groom apparently loved her, and she returned his love. She studied his features. He was shorter than Jake and darker in skin tone. But to her, he was a good-looking, calm, and sweet man.

While taking in the details and arguing in her mind, she was returned to the body. She opened her eyes and looked at me with tears streaming down her cheeks. She never expected all that had happened within few minutes of Earth time but had taken her through events of many years yet to come.

Alice went on to become a changed person. As human beings, we do not like to lose what we cherish. For a while, she tried to hold on to Jake tenaciously, telling herself the spiritual encounter was "Just a vision." But the relationship soon dissolved like ice under the scorching heat. They eventually went their separate ways.

Having been touched by Grace and the Love of the Guardian Angel, she soon became a devoted Christian, volunteering as a worker in the church. This was how she met Tom, who was also a worker. They began a relationship and soon got married. They now have three kids with a boy coming first, followed by a girl as it was shown to her by the Guardian Angel.

God Did Not Make Religions

You must also have noticed the people I speak of come from different religious backgrounds. Religion is a means developed by man in his genuine attempt to understand life and God. God did not make religions.

Man did. God only made mankind in Its image and likeness. That is the most beautiful and most powerful thing in the universe.

Anyone can have contact with the Guardian Angels. You, too, can. It is part of your spiritual heritage.

Contrary to what some charlatans have fed into our minds for ages, God, the Holy Spirit, Grace, visions, prophecies, and miracles are NOT the exclusive preserves of a set of people. God made us with the same potential. However, what we do with the potentials is determined by ourselves.

Anyone can enter the sacred space of Spirit, whether they have a religion or not, whether they are 'holy' or 'just human'. Most times, those who are 'just human' have a better opportunity to enter that sacred space.

DAY TWENTY-ONE

FAITH AND GRATITUDE

Today is the final day of our 21-day journey. As you wake, fill your heart with gratitude to the Source for the blessings you have received in the last twenty days. It is an essential part of a successful and happy life to take stock of all you have received.

It is easy to complain about the things we do not have. We all have an endless list of that. But the list of blessings, Grace, and Mercy is longer and eternal.

Read and Review

Today is a Saturday (if you followed our schedule). You should wake up relaxed and ready to write in your SEJ, your encounters of the night. After doing that, sit back or lie down and read or review all you have recorded in the last twenty days.

While reading or listening to your recordings, fill your heart with love for God, your Guardian Angel, and all of life. While you are reading, quietly sing any of the sacred Words.

Also, place your attention on your Guardian Angel. Imagine they are there listening to your reading. Try to see and hear them, especially when you get to places or points that bring smiles to your face or issues that remain confusing. They will talk to you.

Be Grateful

Today, ask for nothing but just read, review, understand, and be grateful. You must have gotten answers to your questions before today. So, just relax and reflect on all that has happened, both physically and spiritually.

If you are yet to have a direct and conscious spiritual encounter, do not worry. It will come to your awareness as the days go by. Your life will run better and you will be happier, now that you have opened the line of communication with God, Spirit, and the Angels. You can never be the same again.

Gratitude, a Great Prayer Mode

After reviewing your journal, continue with gratitude for life anywhere you go. Prayer is a mode or means of communicating with God. Gratitude is one of the best prayer modes, next to singing sacred Words, which is also a means of gratitude by calling or praising God using Its true spiritual Names, rather than call It 'God' or other names given It by man. These Words are building blocks of Creation.

A More Spiritual You

The spiritual techniques in this book are designed to help you become a better and more spiritual person. Whatever your religion, you must have become a better Christian, Muslim, ECKist, or Buddhist. If you have no religion, you will be operating at the highest level you have ever been. And if something propels us to manifest goodness and God-ness in ourselves, why should we stop? Even though you have seen your future or received answers to what troubles your heart, these techniques will continue to serve you.

Same Gene with God

You are in the image and likeness of God. That means you are the same family, of the same genetic code, same properties as God.

If you realize and become one with this truth, then seeing the future, keeping the company of Guardian Angels, and being bathed in the Grace, Love, Music, and Blessings of Spirit become your second nature.

Light and Waves of Love

After faithfully practicing Soul-Fullness for twenty days, your health, career, relationship, marriage, and peace of mind must have improved greatly. When we communicate with Spirit and the Angels, we tap into the infinite blessings contained in the Ocean of God's Love. These blessings come in the form of Light and waves of Love. These powers bring healing to us and positive transformation in us. Spirit decides which area of our life needs changing, cleansing, uplifting, and healing.

The Power of Love and Wisdom

Love and wisdom are important aspects of these blessings. Most of our ills and challenges are due to inadequate love and wisdom on our part. No matter how knotty a situation is, if we apply the right amount of love and wisdom, an easy solution can be found. Our lives are a series of choices, tests, and trials. A happy and successful person is one who makes the best choices and can face challenges wisely and lovingly. As we have discovered, wisdom, love, and power come from Spirit.

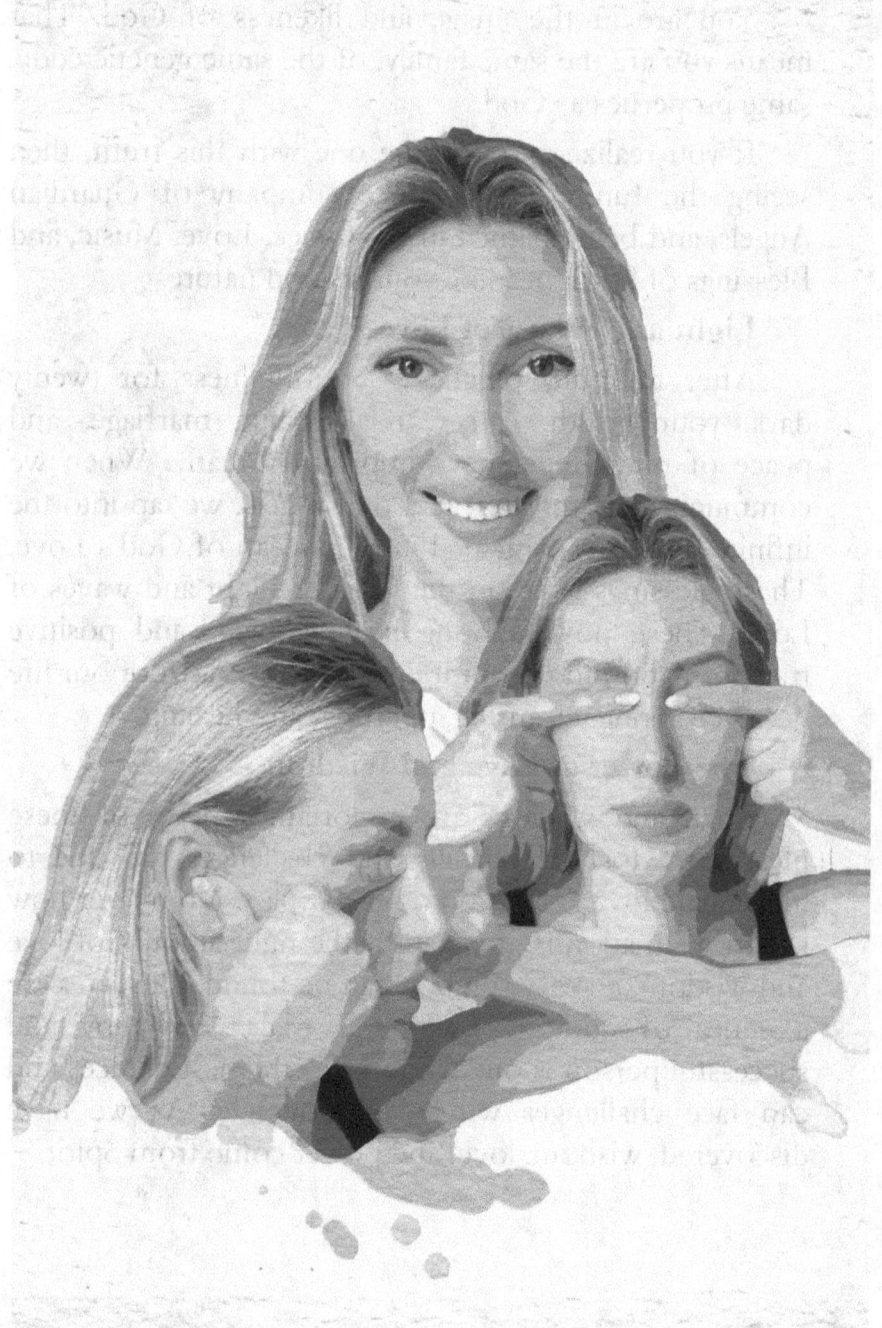

SOUL-FULLNESS

PRINCIPLES

Soul-Fullness is both the process and the essence of operating from the viewpoint of Soul. Since each one of us is Soul, Soul-Fullness can be defined as seeing, hearing, and acting as Soul, our true identity. Acting in this way, adopting the Soul perspective in all things and situations, automatically brings an awareness of certain innate power, creativity, and freedom that the mind, logic, culture, tradition, and society cannot give us. Soul-Fullness, the 21-day program, is a tool to assist us become aware of our true nature and some of the privileges that come with that identity.

In this book I have placed attention on some inner and physical benefits. These include wisdom from Spirit, protection, healing, prophecy, gratitude, forgiveness, and a loving heart, journeys to the invisible realms, keeping the company of Guardian Angels, and the seeing and hearing abilities of Soul. There are more benefits that you will discover as you continue to apply this 21-day technique to your life.

It is pertinent I give you some principles guiding the art and science of Soul-Fullness, with emphasis on the alchemy of life-transformation, dreams, and prophecy. Some are stated below. They should be taken seriously. I have narrated some spiritual encounters to illustrate these principles.

1. Silence

All revelations are for our spiritual growth. It is an intimate relationship between Spirit and us. It is personal and we should keep it so.

2. Show Them the Ropes

Some people use spiritual knowledge as a means of control. Most people, even leaders, are too lazy to accept their own spiritual responsibilities. They run to self-styled prophets and psychics to know who to marry, when to make love to their spouses, travel, run for elections, etc. They are perpetually at the mercy of these so-called gurus who run practically every area of their lives.

This is spiritual slavery and exploitation. It is better to learn how to take your own spiritual decisions and allow others to do the same. Otherwise, you will be subject to the law that commands that you inherit the troubles of the people whose lives you are trying to control.

3. Love and Right Action Are Paramount

Constant practice of these twin virtues will bring a rosy future. It may not necessarily bring fortune, fame, and good health, but it will bring peace of heart or spiritual liberation, which supersedes everything.

4. Faith

If Spirit has given you a revelation, it will come to pass if you keep it to yourself and work towards it. You must have complete faith in your Guardian Angel and Spirit.

THE JOB HUNT

After graduating from the university and I had finished the one-year compulsory national service, the family was once again on my case. Everyone wanted me to work where they were working, but I knew Spirit had a plan for me. I sang the sacred Word and requested to see where I was to work. I had a prophetic dream in which I was in an office complex, and I saw the nameplate of my boss.

About six months later, I attended an interview in that company, but I was not taken. Because of the precognition, I was emboldened to go back to take interviews for other positions. I met with the Chairman and the General Manager, whose initials I had seen written on her door in the spiritual encounter six months earlier. They assessed me and concluded that the first interview panel committed an error of judgment by not employing me *ab initio*. I was subsequently employed.

I worked extra hard to fulfill my destiny in the company, which was a publishing house. A few months later, the editor was fired for poor performance. I was promoted Acting Editor over and above my seniors.

When it was also time to leave, my Guardian Angel gave me specific instructions to that effect. I subsequently put in my resignation, to the utter consternation of my bosses, colleagues, and family. But you must have faith and follow Spirit's directions, boldly and happily, even though on the surface it may appear you are being irrational.

This is one of the reasons you must keep these revelations to yourself. Imagine telling your family you are resigning because of a dream. They will likely organize a prayer session or deliverance for you. That is if they do not send you for psychiatric evaluation first.

After a few months, I got a similar job with better conditions. I was also led to it by the Guardian Saints.

5. Discipline

Can you handle it? If you cannot, then you have lost the trust of Spirit and your Guardian Angel because revealing a future reality is to help you walk towards it boldly, courageously, and lovingly. The same applies to insight given to help you resolve a crisis.

MY MOM'S DEATH

At 14, I began having spiritual encounters in which it was revealed my mom was going to die. She was in her mid-forties. It was hard to handle, especially knowing I could not and must not discuss it with her or Dad. It took three years before she died. It was earth-shattering, but the repeated prophetic dreams had helped to prepare me for the inevitable. I got closer to her during that period of Grace and showed her as much love as I could for three years before she died.

BANK JOB ENDS

Six months before the physical event, I was told in the Heavens that my bank job would soon come to an end and that I must not take another. I was to go into writing to help humanity. I asked to be allowed to combine both, but it did not work. I could not write anything while working in a bank. I left and was guided slowly, even though painfully, to writing these books, after writing a couple of movies, TV dramas, and creating and hosting a TV show.

Life was more challenging, but I had to resist the temptation and pressure to go back to a regular life, which I had enjoyed thoroughly but had kept me away from my destiny and spiritual assignments.

6. Parallel Universes

We are living parallel lives here, and in the First, Second, Third, and Fourth Heavens. An incident may happen in a parallel universe to teach us a spiritual lesson. It begins and ends there. For instance, dying in a dream, ferocious animal attacks, and other fear-inducing encounters may be arranged by Spirit or our Guardian to teach us courage and detachment. Once we have learned it, it does not have to happen here.

VICTORIA AND THE DREAM AFFAIR

A friend, Victoria, got it wrong when she accused her man of infidelity because she kept dreaming of meeting a naked girl in his kitchen. She even went as far as talking to church elders to warn him and the sister.

It never happened in the physical. But the lady had feelings for Victoria's man. Whenever she was out of the body in the dream, she went to the spiritual counterpart of the man's house to show him love. But you cannot tender that as grounds for divorce, just as you cannot arrest a man for robbery because he robs you in a dream.

Victoria got it wrong. She did not realize Spirit was giving her lessons in detachment, which involved rising above jealousy and being able to discipline her mind.

This apparent spiritual indiscipline led to the end of her relationship.

7. The Lesson Is for You

This is the principle that Victoria was yet to learn. It is always for your personal benefit, except in cases of global or group prophecies given to a savior or someone responsible for the group, organization, family, or planet. If not, it is always on a personal and individual level.

The Book of Prophecies contains examples of group or global revelations passed through someone who has been given the responsibility to be of help to the whole. This is done at the instance of Spirit.

8. You Can Change It

By generating love in place of hate, charity instead of selfishness, education and wisdom instead of ignorance, gratitude rather than greed, an undesirable future can be changed to a rosier one. Singing a sacred Word connects us to Spirit, which comes in waves of Light, Music, and Love that transform us, uplifting everyone and everything in the world. We rise higher, beyond our weaknesses.

9. Seek the Realm of the Saints

Look for revelations that will help you help others. Be a servant of life; be of service to life.

THE PROPHETESS

A popular actor's wife, in the middle of a family conversation, looked at me and said, "You know, God is going to use you to help millions of people." She was very sensitive to spiritual realities. I thanked her and appreciated her service as an open channel for Spirit.

Of course, I had known before I was nine years old; but it was reassuring hearing it from someone who only knew me socially. She was expressing a spiritual reality. She was not talking from the mind, but Spirit spoke through her.

10. Do Not Limit Spirit

You may ask for salt and get sugar. Always be ready for a surprise. No worries though, your Guardian's got your back.

Before we came to Earth, we all chose a path to take. Some of us chose certain lessons that may be regarded as suffering from a human perspective. However, from a higher spiritual level, these lessons are seasonings for a good meal. Gold must pass through fire for its inner beauty to manifest. For this reason, we may pray for sugar, but Spirit knows we are better off with bitters. Once we surrender to the Source, Spirit, Allah, Jesus, Mahanta, Rama, Krishna, Jehovah, Chineke, Oludumare, or Sat Nam, then we must be ready to accept what comes as the best for us.

BEYOND PROPHECY

Live a happy, giving, and detached present. You will have a great future.

At a time, I outgrew the need to see the future. It could take the wind out of the sails or dry out the passion. Do not live in the future because the present determines the future. Live a great present and it will continue to be great, no matter the challenges.

Take every action asking, "What will my Guardian Angel say or do were they in my shoes?" And guess what? They have walked this road before, and they have been in our shoes. They know where and how the shoe pinches. They also overcame the temptations and the pain but rose above the allure of the flesh to become one with Spirit. So, think about them before, during, and after any action.

SPIRITUAL EYE TECHNIQUE (SET)

This technique was developed thousands of years ago by the Saints. It is for seeing into the Realms of Soul, seeing the future, and having vivid dreams that involve consciously being in Spirit. I will advise you to do it after singing a sacred Word, especially HU; but Jesus, Allah-HU, HU-Mana, Rama, Shanti are all sacred Words. The name of a Saint is also sacred. The key part to using a sacred Word is to see the image of the Saint or Guardian Angel and fill your heart with love for all of life.

After singing for about ten minutes, breathe in and hold your breath. While holding your breath, place a finger each on the eyelids and gently press them inwards. Not hard, just gently, not to the point of pain. Hold your breath while the fingers are on the eyelids. Release your breath after a minute. Continue to hold the fingers in place while breathing in and out normally.

While in this position, place attention at the Spiritual Eye, the spot where the two eyebrows meet. At first, you might see only a blank screen or darkness, but soon enough you will begin to see pinpoints of light that sometimes grow into a kaleidoscopic array of bright and colorful lights.

After holding the fingers in place for three to five minutes, you may remove them. Continue to stare at the Window of Soul. Be as relaxed as possible. You can lie in bed or on a comfortable surface while doing the SET.

While staring at this Window of Heaven, many have reported seeing Guardian Angels or a scene in the future or in another world. Others find themselves in the Heavens with the Guardian Saint, experiencing the Glory of God vividly. Within a split second of Earth time, you could have an encounter that seems to last a whole day.

Some people do not see beyond the Light, but their level of wisdom becomes manifold.

Do this once a day before you sleep or when you

wake in the middle of the night. When you sleep, you will be amazed at the vividness of your spiritual encounters in the Heavens. Your dreams will graduate from jumbled to meaningful, from symbolic to direct, needing no interpretations.

The SET is a special gift from the Council of Saints to humanity. Do it with love and gratitude. I am sure you remember doing this as a child. It was supposedly a plaything, but the knowledge came from your Guardian. This kept you in touch with the Heavens. Until you began attending schools where 'childish' playthings were frowned at and discouraged. But Jesus said unless you become like a child, did he not? This technique is one of the forgotten gifts of childhood.

With SET your ability to operate from the pedestal of Soul-Fullness expands tremendously. This is equivalent to knocking on the Door of Soul, and using the right key to open it, every night.

NEXT

From this night, let the SET be a regular, once-a-night technique. And from today, or when you deem it fit, go back to **Day One** to set a new spiritual goal of 21 days. Make sure you do all the disciplines but add the sacred Words as part of your daily routine.

You can move to a higher level of Soul-Fullness, which is to seek direct God Wisdom in your daily life to make better decisions, be it in your career, relationship, or health. God is waiting to give once you ask.

I wish you the Grace and Blessings flowing like a massive waterfall, coming from the Throne of Grace, upon your head and into your spiritual heart.

AFTER THE BOOK

SPIRITUAL ENCOUNTERS

After the first edition (*See Your Future in 21 Days*) hit the stores we went on a promotional drive. We visited media houses, students' associations, several professional bodies, restaurants, and even barbers and cosmetologists. During these interactions, I was privileged to have met so many people desirous of the spiritual life. Almost everyone displayed a keen and unalloyed interest in improving their lives. Not everyone wanted a spiritual solution to their problems. Many were attached to their religions and would not entertain anything beyond what their leaders had prescribed as gospel truth.

Beneficiaries of Spirit's Wisdom and Grace

Among the group of the bold, who were willing to consider a fresh angle to life, we discovered several women and men who had some captivating experiences to share with us. Some of these wonderful people had been relating so intimately with Guardian Angels and Spirit physically, in dreams and in the Heavens for a long time. Many of them were aware of these intimate interactions, some were not. But both groups knew they were beneficiaries of God's Wisdom and Grace, and it showed in their lives.

One thing that made them stand out was how their

eyes lit up when they saw the book. The other indicator was how they smiled a secret but knowing smile whenever I looked at them and began talking about the possibilities of seeing the future and hearing from Spirit and Guardian Angels, irrespective of their social, educational, or religious status. It was a magical moment whenever I discovered that here before me was someone who had secretly been having intimate spiritual encounters but had been reluctant to share them with any other person, for the fact that they did not want to be regarded as crazy by their peers and the society at large. In this chapter, I will share stories of six of such people. In the future, we hope to collate other people's experiences as the fulcrum of another book so that the world can share.

"YOU WILL DIE SOON"

Martin was, by all standards, a very practical, down-to-earth man. How would he not be, with a Ph.D. in Physics and Engineering? He was known in Africa, Europe, Asia, and America as a prolific inventor, a university don, organizer of conferences, and a very friendly man without any airs. Personally, I had witnessed him park his SUV by a service station to ride a bike or take a bus just because that was the most convenient thing to do when there was a traffic gridlock. Not a few times did he unsettle his colleagues with this carefree attitude. But Martin could not be bothered by any of that. In every situation, he chose the most practical and the most cost-effective way out.

"The rest is vanity," he would readily reply. "I'm an engineer; what works is more important to me than what is socially and politically correct."

The Invisible Messenger

One day, a few years before we met, he had been standing at a bus stop waiting for a cab under the hot sun when he heard a voice close to his right ear. He turned swiftly to see who was standing behind him. Turning around, he saw no one close enough to have sneaked up behind him to be able to whisper into his right ear.

Not satisfied with what he saw, he turned around, full circle, taking in all the details of human and vehicular movements anywhere close enough to have produced the whisper which, apparently, was meant for him alone and was disturbing, to say the least.

"You will die soon," was the cryptic message he was given by the disembodied voice.

"I reject it," he said out loud, reacting for the first time when it was obvious to him this was a personal message delivered not by physical means but by a mysterious entity that seemed to be on a mission to put an end to his life.

"I reject it!" he said again, this time mustering a lot of courage and passion. "And back to sender, whoever you are. I am not going to die soon. My life is not in your hands. My life is in God's hands only."

He went on with the denunciations, right there at the bus stop. Soon, he was beginning to draw attention to himself, so he had to walk away from the spot, which was turning into a spiritual battle zone. The person he battled was unknown and invisible. He began wondering about the reality of the whole encounter. As an engineer, you must have verifiable proof for every theory, concept, and experience. But this was not in the realm of physics. This was metaphysics. But as far as that pseudo-science was concerned, Martin had no iota of respect for it.

Between Physics and Metaphysics

He went home a very troubled man. Why should he worry, you say? After all, an engineer does not believe it if he cannot prove it with the laws of physics? That would have been applicable were he in another clime. Martin hailed from a place where the psychic art of black magic was as common as buying grocery from the neighborhood store. No one born and bred in these parts would pretend they had not heard, even if they had not seen, people being called to their death while sleeping in their bed. In some cases, it was even alleged a man could be in his office doing his regular duties, and suddenly he would hear a voice calling his name. If he made the mistake of answering out loud, he would either drop dead on the spot or turn insane.

In fact, anytime I visited the place, I never failed to notice a disturbing phenomenon of parents shouting their children's names at least three times before the child would answer. It took a while before a friend reminded me of what the Yoruba call *apeta*. To avoid falling victim to black magicians who had supposedly perfected the art of 'calling' someone to his death with invisible powers, every parent taught their wards not to answer at first call. Three times was a good time to respond to a call. The belief was that the black magician would not be able to send the evil arrow once he had called once or twice and the target had deflected it by not answering.

If you are having a laugh, it is because you have not been exposed to the experiences of people from Martin's homestead. So, you can imagine how palpable the fear that gripped him after the 'death sentence' experience. Yes, he was not a religious man. In fact, going to church was a casual affair for him. He was a man who believed in the practicality of everything. But after this afternoon, he had to take his spiritual survival more seriously.

He consulted some pastors who asked him to embark on several days of white fasting, and to rebuke the devil as often as possible. He complied with all the instructions and directions. In fact, he became more religious than he could have thought possible. But after doing all, he still had the nagging feeling that something tragic was going to happen. He could feel it in his marrow. But he never expected it to come the way it did.

The Accident

He had taken a trip to Lagos and was returning to his base. It was one of those days he had ditched his car for a commercial bus, a minivan sitting fourteen people. The ride was smooth, and he was looking forward to getting home and preparing for the following day's work. It was about 8 p.m. when they turned off the highway onto a four-lane road that led to his city. From that point, it is usually a thirty minutes' drive. Most passengers would be preparing to disembark. Some would use the opportunity of the fresh air supplied by the heavy foliage on both sides of the road to relax their nerves and even take a short nap.

That was what Martin was doing when, suddenly, he had a jolt that came from somewhere within the Spirit. Something was wrong. Something was not right with the way the vehicle was moving. He opened his eyes and raised his head to look around. The vehicle was traveling on the wrong side of the road! From what he could discern, the right side of the road, where they should have been, was closed to traffic. It was under repairs. So, all the vehicles had to be diverted to the left side of the road.

But that was not what was wrong. The vehicle was cruising at top speed, Martin observed. Still, that was not the most crucial problem that could be giving him a bone-chilling feeling of an impending disaster. He craned his neck and peered into the distance. Now, he saw the problem. Both headlamps of the bus were off!

"Driver, what happened to your headlamps?"

The driver barely grunted to acknowledge Martin. So, he had to try again, a little more forcefully. "Put on your headlamps! How can you be driving on the wrong side of the road without lights, in a dark place like this?"

"I don't know what happened; the lights went off just now," the driver shot back angrily.

Martin could scarcely believe his ears. The headlamps had burned out. The vehicle was on the wrong side of the road facing oncoming vehicles that were in their own regular lane. And to worsen the matter, he was driving at top speed. Nothing could be a more effective way to court disaster. What further irked him was that the other passengers did not utter a word of complaint. Neither did they support his efforts to slow down the driver.

Just about a minute into the altercation with the driver, it happened. The only thing he saw was the raised hood of the heavy truck broken down beside the road. The last thing he heard was a deafening bang. He lost consciousness after that.

Back from the Dead

When he opened his eyes to behold this world, it was about three days after the accident. He was at the ICU of the Federal Medical Center. When he took in his surroundings and his body, he noticed he had a nagging headache and several stitches on his head and neck where he had sustained multiple injuries. The doctor and the nurses attending to him were obviously joyous that he had regained consciousness.

"Was everybody drunk or asleep in the bus, that no one could tell the driver he was driving in the night without any lights?" one of the nurses enquired.

"I told him. He wouldn't listen, and the other passengers said I was talking like the only wise man on board."

"That's unfortunate, because everyone died. You're the only survivor."

Martin was jolted to full wakefulness with that revelation. His mind went back to the mysterious whispering he had spent days on end praying and fasting against. The plan of the evil one seemed to have come close to materializing. He would have died like the rest.

While he narrated his experience, I listened intently, learning, and looking for pointers from Spirit. Martin was sure the enemies had engineered the whole accident. To him, it was an attack by the devil, probably sent by some adversaries that wanted his downfall.

We can never rule out the hand of the envious adversaries at any time in our lives. However, the voice that whispered into his ear, giving him a prophecy foretelling his imminent death, was an act of Grace given by Spirit through his Guardian Angel. Without the warning, he would have gone on with life in his usual devil-may-care attitude. He would not have given more attention to the spiritual part of himself, which helped him to be vigilant and to also earn several positive spiritual points. This helped to halt his unmitigated ride into the land of the dead, unlike the others.

How to Change Bad Prophecy

A question arose while we were deliberating. How can you change an unpleasant prophecy or reverse a revelation that appears inimical to our comfort and well-being?

The first point to hold on to tenaciously is the one I just stated. Revelations, visions, or divine Wisdom are not of our making. They are acts of Grace from God to us. So, if it is going to happen, it will happen. But if God reveals it to us, it is an opportunity to move to a higher rung of the survival ladder. If we have developed an intimate relationship with our Guardian Angel, and we are used to communicating in a crystal-clear fashion, we would know the next line of action when the revelation is given. See the chapter 'Soul-Fullness' for more on this.

Ask for Divine Guidance

An effective technique is to sit down in your prayer chair and sing HU for about ten to fifteen minutes. And, as I have said repeatedly, you can sing JEEE-SUS, ALLAH-HU, or RAA-MAA, depending on what you find agreeable. While at it, review the revelation and go into a conversation (in the mind) with your Guardian Angel, and ask for divine guidance. Remain quiet for about ten minutes while listening with the Inner Ear and watching with the Inner Eye for any messages from Spirit.

Usually, Spirit will respond. However, if you do not receive any direct message, then imagine you are standing by a river flowing with white light instead of ordinary water. Take the image of the unpleasant prophecy and throw it into the river. See it dissolve, and then (from the same River of Light) imagine and retrieve the most pleasing version of the events as you desire.

Surrender to God

Be positive; be creative. Do not spend (or waste) energy rebuking the devil or the enemies. That is not your concern. It should not be. Your focus should be on God, Spirit, and the betterment of your life.

After about ten minutes of recreating the future, then surrender it to God: "May Thy Will be done." It is hard to do, but it MUST be done. Otherwise, you are trying to fight a war that you cannot win. It is God's battle; it is not yours.

You can repeat this sequence in the morning and in the evening every day, for as long as you feel it is necessary.

GUNNERS FOR LIFE!

Moses is a self-driven, adventurous Ghanaian friend of mine. At a relatively young age, he packed a small bag and headed out of Accra. Destination? Unknown. He just wanted a new lease on life, and wherever fate took him, he was game. After hopping from one major city to another in West Africa, he ended up in Nigeria. This was how we met.

Before the book was written, we both attended workshops on spiritual subjects. It was at one of these meetings that we got talking about Soul-Fullness and the possibilities of being your own prophet, severing the penchant to be dependent on some know-it-all charlatans. I shared the Spiritual Eye Technique with him, but I never asked him how or what he did with it.

The month the book was released, we met again in my office. I had two other guests who were skeptical about the stories and techniques in the book. That was when Moses, in an uncharacteristic manner, opened up without being prompted. Usually, he was a little laid-back and shy when it came to speaking in a place populated by unfamiliar faces.

"It works; it really works," was how he came in.

"Are you sure?" queried Happiness, on record as the first buyer of the book, an intelligent, self-confident mother of two lovely children. She was not the type to readily believe anything out of the ordinary.

"Yes, Madam. It works like magic," Moses said, with emphasis.

And the Winner Is...

Looking at his ebony face, punctuated by snow-white teeth and bright eyes, I knew he had more to say. "Go ahead, Moses. Tell us your story."

"Remember the last FA Cup final between Hull and Arsenal?"

"Yes, I do. What happened?"

"You know everyone thought Arsenal wouldn't win the cup. Even when the match was ongoing, it looked like Hull had it wrapped up until the table turned."

"Yes, I remember. So, what's that got to do with this Spiritual Eye Technique?"

"I knew Arsenal was going to win. I knew as early as 3 a.m."

"Interesting. How did you know that?"

"Before I slept, I'd done the SET. As I slept, I found myself in a stadium, the FA Cup final was about to be played. I saw the flags of both teams standing side by side. Then I asked my Master, who is a Guardian Angel, who would carry the Cup. He didn't answer me. He just pointed to the two flags. So, I kept looking. Suddenly, the flag of Arsenal began rising higher and higher until it dwarfed that of Hull's. The meaning was very clear to me. I knew my team would win."

"Wonderful. So, what did you do when you woke up?"

"You know people bet a lot, and they wanted me to bet. Everyone was betting against Arsenal. In fact, if I hadn't had the prophetic dream, I would have bet against Arsenal."

"So, you made a lot of money betting Arsenal?" Happiness asked with an expectant smile.

Moses laughed. "No, I didn't do any betting. My Master wanted to save me from losing money, that's why he showed me the winner of the match. It wouldn't be right to now use that spiritual revelation to make money out of others."

The techniques in this book work. But they work better for your spiritual growth and overall well-being when you do them with complete faith and reliance on the true Agents of Spirit. Your motives must be noble. Your heart must be pure. Your goal must never be to take advantage of others. Otherwise, the techniques would stop working, and the Law of Karma would take its course.

"YOUR LORDSHIP"

I was in a barber's shop when the gangling, 15-year-old young man entered. He was so tall he had to bend to avoid his head touching the ceiling fan. The guys there, who were quite familiar with him, laughed as if on a prompt. I did not get the joke at first until I took a closer look at his face, which showed his youthfulness and the fact that he was yet to reach his zenith as far as vertical elongation of the bones was concerned.

Later, I asked Peter (not his real name) if he played basketball.

"No, Sir," he responded in a tone of respect coupled with the gesticulations of someone brought up in a conservative environment.

"Why is that?"

"My dad won't let me."

"Serious? Then let me talk to him on your behalf. You shouldn't be wasting this tall and athletic body. Maybe he's afraid you won't be serious with your studies once you start playing."

"I'm serious with my books. I even promised him he should make me stop if my grades dropped."

"That's a good deal. Why is he adamant?"

"I Am Going to Be a Judge"

There was a whimsical, puzzled expression on his face for a second before it vanished. Long enough for me to notice there was something he was not sure he should tell me. "Go ahead, Peter, say it."

"He knows I'm going to be a judge."

I studied his face to be sure he was not putting me on. "Tell me the story."

"About four years ago, I was given a revelation. It was in the day, like a vision. I saw myself in a courtroom. There were lawyers and many cases were being tried in the court. I was the judge. The lawyers were bowing to me, calling me, 'Your Lordship'. It was so real. It wasn't a dream."

"That's a good one. So, you told Daddy. That's why he doesn't want you to play basketball?"

"Yes. I have to study Law. It's a tough course. I must be serious."

"Yes, I know. But that shouldn't stop you from playing basketball. In fact, being engaged in a competitive game like basketball will not only be good for your body, but it will sharpen your mind. It will help you become a great lawyer and, eventually, a great judge."

"Is that so?"

"Yes, Peter. You know what? Tell Daddy you met a man who says he should please allow you to play basketball as long as you follow your dream of reading Law."

"Thank you, Sir. I will tell him."

He did as agreed, but Daddy stuck to his guns. Then I did what he was not expecting. I wrote him a letter. I explained that life is a series of events that are connected. Some people have labeled it 'connecting diamonds'. Everything is related. And, if we allow ourselves to be guided by Spirit, we will follow the trail, trusting that we are on the right path to greatness.

To Peter's joy and my relief, his dad agreed to allow him play basketball on weekends and during holidays. Fair enough.

Because the Spirit reveals that you will someday become the president of America does not mean you pack all your load and start camping in front of the Whitehouse. In fact, you may have to be a janitor somewhere in Arizona first and do all you need to do to earn enough experience and good points to deserve the opportunity to serve at that level.

BARBER, SCULPTOR, AND PART-TIME PROPHET

Hassan does not look like the regular Islamic cleric. He is tall, wears jeans and a shirt, and is clean-shaven. At the time we met, he was the outgoing president of the barbers' association of his State, a body comprising thousands of members.

But the first pointers that this was not a regular guy were the imposing sculptures adorning half of his business space, while the barbing shop took the rest. They called him Alhaji Hassan. You could see the women and men with whom he regularly interacted had so much respect for him, his boyish looks and carefree appearance, notwithstanding.

We had booked an appointment with him to discuss the book and the possibility of making a presentation to his body of members. I watched closely as my colleague, Balo, presented him with a copy. He looked at the book and asked for a presentation. Since Balo was also a Muslim, I thought he was the best person to talk to Hassan, especially in the Yoruba language.

It went well. However, I noticed Hassan had more to share. While Balo was making his presentation, Hassan was cracking one joke after another with the aim of putting everyone at ease. This convivial atmosphere helped a lot. I could see his heart radiated a lot of Light. So, I threw in a line.

"Alhaji Hassan, I can see you're very familiar with the subject of the book."

He looked at me with a smile playing at the corners of his mouth. "Why did you say that, Sir?"

"I see you're a barber and a very good sculptor. And

I know as an artist, inspiration only comes from the Spirit. You must have had several prophetic and revelatory visions and dreams to be able to come up with all these good stuff."

He looked at me once again, and, for the first time, he dropped the front of the simple, jocular character. "You're not wrong, Sir. I will read the book and we will discuss. In fact, I promise to study it, and I'll make notes to show you when we meet."

"The Best Book on the Subject"

A month later, Hassan sent us an invitation to attend a general meeting of the association. When we arrived at the venue, I could see he liked the book and had done a lot of groundwork, talking to the key officers.

I spoke to the house for about five minutes. I felt it went well, but Hassan took over and spoke for fifteen minutes, during which I came close to tears.

"I've read so many books on spiritual topics: Christian, Buddhist, Sufi, *Ifa*, Lobsang Rampa, and so on. But this book is the best I've read on this topic. If you read it, your life will never be the same again. After studying it, I followed the 21-day program as directed by the writer. In fact, I was transported into the Heavens. Several *Malaikas* spoke to me in the dream. One even asked me to stop eating fish and meat for a while. I've complied."

He paused to gauge the reaction of his audience, many of whom belonged to the diverse and divergent spiritual traditions he had mentioned. Telling them that here was a book that impressed him as much as the ones he had read, if not more, was a bold statement to make.

"I've decided that when my daughter turns 16, I'm

going to hand this book over to her. She must read and practice the techniques. Her life will be better guided and happier if she follows the steps here. I tell you this: the writer of this book deserves an award."

Surprise

After such an unexpected, unabashed appraisal in front of a large crowd of young and middle-aged men I was meeting for the first time, I had nothing more to say. I was truly taken aback while wondering which of the Guardian Angels had spoken to Hassan beforehand. I knew there was more to him.

He proved me right when he called me outside to show me his Spiritual Encounter Journal, with entries dating back to three years before we met — three years before he read about it in my book.

"I am impressed with all this. It shows Guardian Angels have been relating with you and guiding you for a very long time."

Point of Disagreement

"Yes. The *Malaikas* used to give me messages for others. It started about seven years ago. Almost every night, I receive one message or the other, either for myself or for people I know. That's why the only point of disagreement between me and your book is the law that forbids giving a message to another person. These messages have saved lives. They've helped many people turn their lives around for the better."

I took a deep breath and examined the facts of his case. In the principle he was referring to, I stated that it is better you teach others how to see their future rather than turn yourself into a small god. It leads to servitude on one hand, and karmic burdens on the other. But there is always an exception, and I explained to him.

"As a rule, you don't go around revealing the contents of your dreams and revelations. It will be vain to do so. But when you've developed a closer relationship with your Guardian Angel, he or she may give a specific message for someone close to you, someone that needs urgent help but might not be open enough to Spirit to receive it directly.

"Most times, the message must have been given to the person concerned, but a third party may be necessary to confirm or convince the person that their dreams or visions are not fantasies. There must also be a spiritual tie between you and the person. They may be family or friend, even dating back to another life before this one.

"However, before you give such a message to anyone, or any time you receive a revelation concerning another person, sing HU for about two minutes and say, "God, direct me." You will receive guidance."

A radiant smile creased his boyish face. "Thanks for clarifying that. It looks like our point of disagreement no longer exists. I appreciate the vital secrets you just gave me. Without any doubt the *Malaikas* sent you to me."

My personal encounter with Hassan ended with him asking me to demonstrate how to sing HU and the other sacred Words. He was quite familiar with HU because of his background in Sufism, but he wanted to know how I sang it.

As we left the meeting, I was overwhelmed with joy because of the omnipresence of Spirit and the great Souls who guide all of us, irrespective of our religion, ethnicity, or social status. It was made clear to me that Soul-Fullness is universal, especially for those who are ready and sincere to experience the Embrace of Spirit.

TO LONDON WITH LOVE

Mercy had been separated from her husband for about four years. It was not of her making. The British High Commission had simply refused her and her handsome four-year-old son from joining husband and father who was all along based in London while they were in Lagos. She was denied a visa a few times.

When she narrated her plight, I could see the pain she was going through. It was also telling on her nerves. The most excruciating emotion for her was watching her son call every man he saw, "Daddy."

Best for Everyone?

Within me, as she poured her heart out, I sang the Word and asked one of my Guardian Angels: "If it's the best for everyone, may her wish be granted."

This was several months before this book was released. When it came out, she got a copy and read it within a week. She returned feeling ecstatic.

"This book is fantastic, Mr. James. In fact, I was wondering if you were the one who wrote it."

Balo, who was at the meeting, laughed and looked at me. He took the book from her and opened to the author's page. "Didn't you see this page?"

"I saw it, Mr. Balo. But you don't understand what I mean."

Guardian Angels Dictated the Book

I understood what she meant, so I bailed her out. "You're right, Mercy. I also read it a chapter a day like you did, doing the 21-day program repeatedly. Every time I discover something new, something special. The truth is that Spirit and the Guardian Angels used my hand to write it, but they actually wrote it by dictating it to me."

There was total silence from everyone. While they were contemplating the new puzzle I had just introduced, I asked her a more personal question: "So, how did you feel, reading it?"

Loved by God

"I was transported to another world. I did not see anything in particular, but I felt great. I felt peace. I felt loved by God."

I had known her for about a year. Looking at her now, I could see the radiance of someone who had been touched by the Hand of Grace.

"Mercy, that's the most wonderful thing in the world. The prophecies, the visions, the dreams, and the revelations are all good. But they are just the door to the Land of Grace. You have already experienced it. Keep doing the gratitude technique and your life will be full of love, happiness, and Grace."

A month after this encounter, she called to tell me the embassy had granted her visa and they would be moving to London to be a family for the first time since she got married. I was overjoyed for her. The waves of love and happiness she transmitted, even over the phone, were infectious. Silently, I thanked Spirit and the Angels.

RAZAQ GETS HIS MIRACLE

At the time we met, Razaq was a Muslim. By the time he had read and applied the techniques in this book, Razaq got his miracles. He remained a Muslim, but now with a deeper and very practical understanding of how Allah bestows blessings through the Guardian Angels on all those yearning and willing to submit to Him in Spirit.

He was suffering from a debilitating heart condition

that almost incapacitated him at work and at home, pushing him to the precipice of despair. He had visited different specialists in the orthodox medical profession, to no avail. He tried out the *Alfas* in his Islamic faith and herbal medicine practitioners. Without succor, he did the unthinkable for someone with strong religious convictions; he crossed the fence to the other side — attending Christian crusades and prayer sessions in search of a cure. But this proved futile, and soon he became desperate, so he gave voodoo a try. Still, all came to naught. His troubles remained with him.

Total Surrender to the Will of Allah

When it became crystal clear to him that the condition was not going away using all conventional means at his disposal, he resorted to surrendering himself and the condition to Allah. "You give; you take, as it pleases you. If it pleases you, kindly take away this pain."

Unknown to him, he had just applied one of the most powerful spiritual keys: total surrender to the Source. What followed came to him as a strong nudge. He was moved to open up to his barber, a fellow Muslim, and incidentally my barber as well. In a muffled tone laden with emotion, he told of his desperation and how his health condition had almost grounded his business. Would the barber happen to know of any miracle cure that could relieve him of this burden?

God's Ways Are Beyond Our Understanding

Without thinking about it, my barber promptly mentioned my book to Razaq.

"I've not read it. But those who have say the techniques in the book have helped them. You can try it. Who knows, your solution might be there. God's ways are beyond our understanding."

Razaq got a copy of the book. But he had read so many books and had taken so many medications that he had lost hope in books and techniques touted by authors who claimed to be experts, prophets, or specialists. He did not read the book. He returned to my barber the following day.

"I Want to See the Writer"

"I want to see the writer of the book. I don't think I want to read another book. I am tired of searching for a solution inside books. Can you introduce me to the writer?"

"Okay. I will call him and hear what he will say."

After this conversation, I got a call from my barber, telling me Razaq was in urgent and desperate need to talk. I obliged. I subsequently spoke with Razaq. I encouraged him to read the book, a chapter before bedtime. But more importantly, he should sing the Word for fifteen minutes before bedtime and at dawn. This should be accompanied by a silent declaration of total surrender to Spirit.

Dream Mosque and Two Holy Men

Razaq complied. He read the first chapter and sang HU before he slept. Immediately he slept, he found himself in what appeared to be a mosque. Several worshippers were filing out of the main hall after what appeared like the Friday *Jumaat* service was over. The *Alfa* walked up to him and told him to enter an inner room meant for the senior clerics.

Inside the inner room, he saw two elderly clerics seated on their prayer mats, telling their beads. Both were turbaned.

"There was a feeling of holiness that filled the room.

It was coming from these men," recalled Razaq.

At first, the holy men did not mind him; they went on telling their beads, like Muslim clerics do when chanting, 'La ila illalahu' 1111 times. He watched, nonplussed, feeling he had intruded on something so sacred.

While looking from one turbaned man to another, one of them rose, walked up to him. "He was slim, tall, and graceful. His eyes pierced into me like a knife. He had a small sticker in his hands. I don't know where it came from, but I just noticed he was holding it, with his eyes not leaving mine for a moment."

The holy man promptly stuck the sticker-like object to Razaq's chest, over the heart. After a short while, he peeled it off, to Razaq's chagrin, who felt like his heart was being wrenched out of his chest. The elderly cleric directed Razaq to another room, which had been invisible to him.

Holy Shower

Upon entering the second inner room, all he saw was water falling from an invisible shower head. Without any prompting, he stepped under the shower, soaking himself in the water.

"I've never felt so good in my life. As the water touched my body, I felt all the worries, problems, ailments I'd ever had lifting, dissolving and disappearing. I felt great. I felt whole."

The water was the essence of Spirit, cleansing all impurities. It only appeared to Razaq in the form of water because that was the best way he could relate with it at that time. For others, it could appear in the form of Light or even Sound. Some are privileged to see Spirit appearing in the form of a human being, a very holy person. Razaq had experienced Spirit as the two holy men and as the cleansing water.

For those who are interested in conscious exploration of the Heavens, Razaq had journeyed through the First, Second, and Third Heavens. The First Heaven was where the prayer session took place. The inner chamber where the two Guardians sat telling their beads was the Second Heaven, aka Causal Plane. The second inner room where he saw what appeared like water from the shower head was the Third Heaven, otherwise called the Mental Plane. This was where his healing was perfected because it originated in the deep recesses of his mind, dating back to several past lives. One of the holy men was the venerable Shams-i-Tabrizi who serves as a Guardian for all Souls who are ready for God's Love.

Healed!

Razaq woke up to discover the heart condition was gone. He was ecstatic. As a faithful Muslim, he believed in the all-powerful and the all-merciful Allah. "Alhamdu lillahi," he chanted, thanking God for GRACE.

AFTER THE BOOK II

CONVERSATION IN PARADISE ON DEATH AND THE AFTERMATH

The virus code-named COVID-19 did a lot of damage to the human society we had always known. Millions of people died of one complication or another from the disease. Fear, uncertainty, panic, and social upheavals attended the disruption to human culture and lifestyle. America was worst-hit by the pandemic. Living in California, I witnessed, firsthand, the impact of fear and ignorance caused by a dearth of spiritual awareness.

Top on the list of what bothered most of my friends in Los Angeles, as well as New York, two cities that felt the blow more than others, was the age-old existential question: What happens to us when we die?

That question science, psychology and the politicians have not been able to answer. The religionists, who pretend they know, only offer palliatives they have concocted based on snippets found in the writings of prophets and those who have had a close brush with death. While these stories contain fragments of the truth, the whole truth has become muddied and muddled, spiced with wild conjectures, misinformation, misinterpretation, and flight-of-fancy type of fabrication. The result is mass dissemination of untruths and outright falsehoods that only compound the problem for people who have unexpectedly lost their loved ones to the virus.

Sandy, for instance, was a 56-year-old friend whose world turned black when she lost her husband and her only son within the spate of one week. She was inconsolable. I spoke with her a couple of times to give her my condolences and to encourage her as much as I could. After a month, I noticed she was sinking deeper and deeper into depression. I evaluated the situation and decided to tell her about the interview I had with a young lady in the Astral, also known as *Jannah*, Paradise, or the Far Country. When I finished sharing the story, I noticed a glow and spark of hope in her cheeks, eyes, and aura. She smiled and thanked me for pulling her out of a dark place.

Subsequently, I decided to include the story in this book as a bonus, hoping that it will help to allay the fears, lessen the worries, and the feelings of hopelessness that the world had been plunged into since the Coronavirus pandemic. I hope it will be of help to you or someone you know. Do not hesitate to pass it along.

THE MYSTERY OF DEATH AND DYING

In 2015, I had a chat with a lady in the Astral. She had recently died in an automobile accident (in the physical world) at the age of 32 and had left behind two young kids and their father.

I was still on my spiritual retreat, in the pristine village of Arakanga, at the outskirts of Abeokuta in Ogun State, Nigeria. My days and nights were devoted to various spiritual exercises, including mental fasts and deep contemplation. The year 2015 was Year 5 of my agreement with Spirit to undertake this exercise. I had two more years to go.

One of my research interests was death, dying, and how people handle the process, especially immediately after discarding the body. Sounds morbid? Not really. The ignorance surrounding death and dying is largely responsible for the confusion, phobia, attachment to material things and situations, which have precipitated wars, social strife, greed, and the unnecessary acquisition of perishable goods that people erroneously call 'wealth'.

Religious leaders, sociologists, philosophers, and psychoanalysts have only compounded the issue by confusing man a lot more with their wild guesses, suppositions, and embellishments. In the last 5000 years, humanity has been fed with half-baked or badly baked stories of what happens after death, where the Soul goes, and what happens to the individual over time.

A few persons, like my mom, who have had out-of-body experiences, or have been able to consciously visit the other realms, have returned with a more expansive awareness about life. This, in turn, has bolstered their confidence and the need to give more to make life a lot easier for themselves and others. They become heroic in their mindset, actions, and convictions. They are creative. They do not fight or blame anyone for their conditions; rather, they use their Soul Energy to build their own preferred environment. They know they can, and they know how to.

So, in my research into death, dying, and the aftermath, I chose to ask someone who had recently died and was still undergoing the process of settling down in the Astral, a.k.a Paradise. How was the experience of dying or withdrawing from the body? I was also interested in the mental and emotional separation (sense of loss) that the individual must have gone through. Yes, on this side, we know how painful that loss could be on those who were intimate with the departed Soul. But, how about the person who we had supposedly lost? How did they handle it all?

Welcome to Paradise

I was in the Astral fully awake as wakefulness can be. I was in the Soul body but was visible to the inhabitants of this neighborhood because I manifested in a body in tune with Astral vibration and energy. I could have been invisible to the environment, but I needed to relate and have a feel of this place. The environment was like a well-paved street on Earth, with houses of different shapes, trees, and beautiful flowery plants, lining the streets.

But the comparisons ended there.

The trees, flowers, fruits had colors you cannot find on Earth. There were plants that looked like the ones here on Earth, but they had some energy, a heightened vibration to them. The air was filled with vigor, certain buoyancy that cannot be put into human words. The skyline, the horizon, sometimes would change into colors beyond what we see in the physical rainbow. It was like everything had a mind of their own, and they gave out and received currents, energies, that brought peace, love, and heightened appreciation of life.

My job here today was not to savor the environment, eat the almost magical fruits, and hang out with people. No, I had done more than enough of that since I was a lad. As a kid, going to the Astral was my favorite pastime.

I was here to interview someone who had recently relocated from the physical. I had to get on with it because I knew my body was asleep in my room, and I would have to return once the cock crowed, and my neighbor kicked his motorcycle to head out at 5 a.m.

Meet Karen

I 'walked' up to her. She was standing on the porch of this bungalow that looked like a regular three-bedroom house. Even though he did not come outside to say hello, with Soul vision I knew there was a man in the house. I also knew they were living together.

With courtesy, I greeted her. "How are you doing?"

"I am doing fine." Then she smiled. Her smile brought waves of happiness that touched my aura. She was a genuinely loving Soul. In appearance, about 5 feet 5 inches tall, moderate body weight, ebony skin color.

Usually, people who have died will keep the same appearance as they had on Earth until their next incarnation, when they take on a new body. In the case of Karen (not her real name), she might be coming back as a black man or woman, Caucasian, or Indian. When she returns as an Italian male in Milan, for instance, the memories of having been a black woman would be buried deep in the subconscious, but the lessons learned would be available for regular upload.

A few persons do remember but most people will only have vague recollections that burst to the surface when they daydream, sleep, during prayer, or when they go through some traumatic experience. Periods of sharpened intuitiveness, déjà vu, visions, religious experiences, and nightmares provide the outlets for some of these archived memories from our past lives.

On a large scale, most children have vivid recollections of their past lives until they get into high school and the educational system rewires their minds. They become less and less in tune with their higher selves, and more in tune with social dictates.

The Process of Dying

"Tell me; was it painful, dying in that car accident?"

She paused, looked away, and then returned her gaze to meet mine. "Surprisingly, it wasn't painful. Compared to all the fears that I had about death, it was quite smooth."

"Okay; that's comforting." I noticed she had relapsed into a dreamy, reflective state. "I need to know how you felt after detaching from the body."

"At first, there was that pain, not as I knew it on Earth, but that sense of loss."

"Your family?"

"Yes. Especially my children. That took some getting used to. I was first alarmed that I wouldn't see them again. But the Counselors helped me through the transition."

"That sounds good. Tell me more about that."

"They are like guides, or healers, if you will. From the moment I detached from the body, they were always there to help. Just like in a hospital on Earth where you have doctors and nurses that help you heal. The healing process doesn't involve tabs as we used to take on Earth. But there are clinics here where the dislocation created by the shift from Earth to here was rearranged. They also tutored me to adjust to life here. Now, I am at peace with myself."

"Good. But your former children?"

Now, she smiled. "They visit me here. Their dad comes occasionally, but not as often as when I first came. Everyone is learning to move on. He has another lady in his life. She's good to my children. I'm learning not to call them children. We are all equal. But, once a mother, always a mother."

"Do you know whether they remember when they wake up on Earth?"

"That's one of the effects of living on Earth. When they come here, they are alive. We have fun. I sometimes give them vital information on what they need. They will promise me they would do it immediately they get back to the body. But it's always not the case. The Earth brain forgets. It used to bother me when I first got here. I wanted their dad to find some documents that would help them live a better life there. But every time, he would forget. It was disturbing until I learned to let go. It's not that important. Life on Earth is too slow, but it doesn't matter."

I paused. I listened to know if it was time to go back. I had a few moments left. I had to bring this visit to a close. "Thank you for sharing your experience and journey with me. As you know, I am going to write about it so that people on Earth can broaden their worldview on death and life."

"I am happy to help. You are doing something good. I wish I had read such writings as you are doing. It would have helped me prepare for the change."

"Thank you, Karen, for the encouragement. Most people on Earth are too busy chasing after what they don't need to have enough time to read up on what they really need. It's a strange place."

"I know, James; especially now that I am here. I wasted a lot of time on Earth on irrelevant matters.

There Is Nothing to Worry About

"Do you have a last word for my readers?"

She remained quiet. When someone is quiet here, it is

not about making sounds with the mouth. It involves the emotions, the thoughts, and the inflow and outflow of energies through the power channels that we call chakras. I noticed the radiance of her skin as it interacted with the air (not air as we have it here; currents, more or less). She looked like she was 22 years old by human standard, but she had died on Earth at the age of almost 33.

This brought back the memories of when I was 18. One evening my dead mom had entered my room while I was in prayers (chanting Buddhist mantras). She had passed through the wall, with purple-colored energy, or aura, surrounding her, as she appeared to float about two feet from the ground. What was more striking to me was how she had appeared like a 20-year-old even though she had died at 46, eighteen months earlier. To startle me further, she was very trim, wearing long braided hair.

Back to Karen.

"Tell them to worry less. There is nothing to worry about. No matter what you're going through on Earth, it is just a situation; it will change. The universe loves and cares about you more than you can ever imagine."

"Thank you for those beautiful words. I will find a way to tell people on Earth. I must go now. Whenever I come around here in the future, I will say hello."

Back to Earth

Next thing I heard was the loud cock that usually woke me up at 5 a.m. The village Big Ben, I used to call him. He never missed the time.

Going to the other worlds in full consciousness may be as simple as Jesus, Saint Paul, or John did, or as Buddha, Krishna, Shamus-i-Tabriz, and other Saints have done. But you do not have to be a Saint to be able to visit. You do it all the time. You just do not remember all the time.

In parting, I do not recommend the use of drugs to have out-of-body experiences. Truth is, some places are nasty on the other side, just as there are places even more beautiful than where Karen was living. Drugs can open you up to the nasty places. Everything you need to reach the higher universes is inside you, has always been there even before birth.

I hope you use this book to raise yourself to a conscious awareness of your own Soul-Fullness, in principle and in practice.

I wish you the Blessings of the Ancient One!

— *Tosin King James*

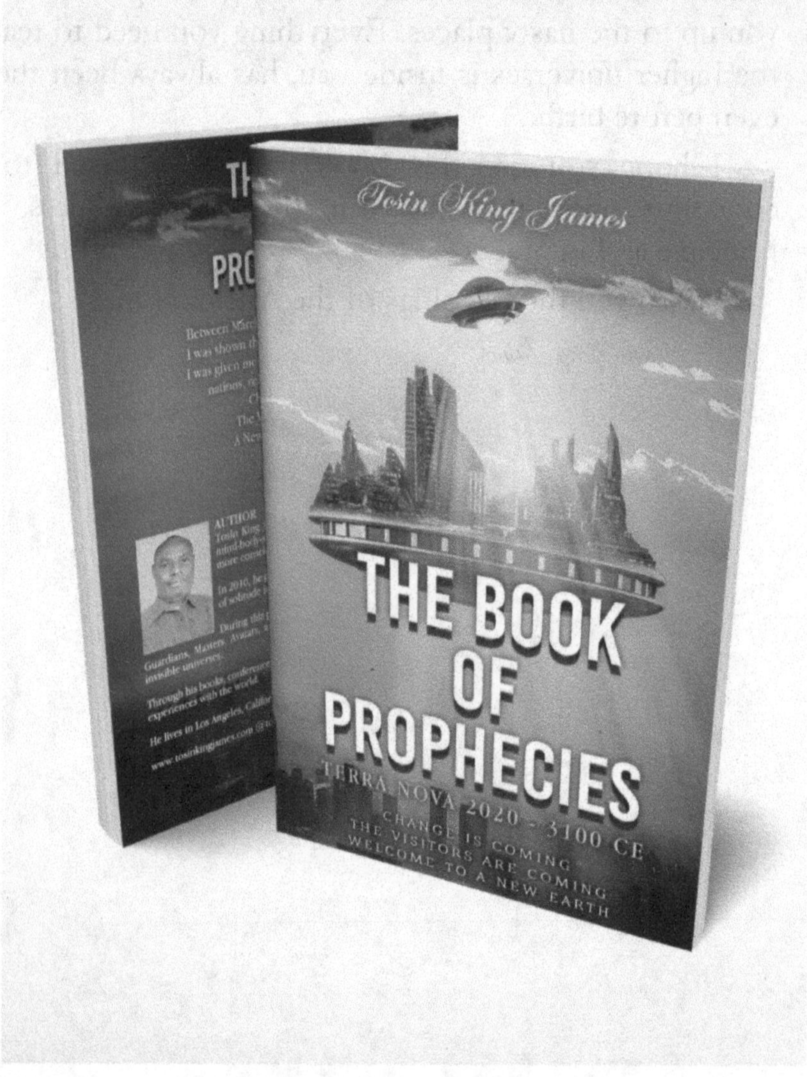
Tosin King James
THE BOOK OF PROPHECIES
TERRA NOVA 2020 - 3100 CE
CHANGE IS COMING
THE VISITORS ARE COMING
WELCOME TO A NEW EARTH

PREFACE TO
THE BOOK OF PROPHECIES
- Terra Nova 2020 - 3100 CE

Almost two thousand years ago, Saint John, the Revelator, was banished to the Island of Patmos as punishment for teaching people the Way to Eternal Life. But solitary confinement turned out to have been a blessing in disguise. It afforded him the ample opportunity to sing the sacred Words unceasingly and to journey into the Heavens in the company of the Lords. Some of his experiences in the First, Second, and Third Heavens, he recorded in *Revelation*. This epochal book reveals the probable future of mankind until about 3000 CE.

It is worthy of note that this book was first rejected by the committee that put together the books to be contained in the Christian Holy Bible. It contained images, symbols, and dramatic events describing a future that must have astounded the minds of scholars and priests at that time. For instance, his description of flying horses and other weird creatures was regarded by more than a few as the nightmares of a lonely old man, suffering the pangs of banishment.

After almost two thousand years and having seen airplanes and other flying objects, John has become more believable in the minds of his followers and critics. He is no longer regarded as a delusional disciple and prophet like he was treated for two millennia.

Self-Banishment

The Book of Prophecies contains revelations, admonitions, and spiritual secrets that might be unbelievable to some scholars and people of faith. However, unlike John's book, we do not have to wait for too long before the events I have recorded here begin to come to pass. Some are already ongoing!

Between March 2010 and September 2017, I was on a self-imposed banishment from the routine of social life. I journeyed in the 'wilderness' to places I had never been and lived in places that were remote and pristine, either by a hill, a river, or in the woods. I was physically and emotionally quarantined from family and friends. I abstained from the pleasures of the mind and body, including sex. I ate fruits, vegetables, and some meat, just enough to sustain the body. At the same time, I spent every minute in contemplation, singing the sacred Words, journeying into the Heavens, the future, the Bosom of God, and communing with the Lords — otherwise called Masters, Saints, Guardian Angels, Avatars, *Malaikas,* or Divine Helpers.

Past Lives and the Book of Records

During this period, some of the content of this book was given to me. Some of it had been revealed to me piecemeal since I was young and before I was born. Yes, I have lived several lifetimes, and I do remember essential details from some of them. In the past, I have been Scottish, English, French, Italian, Jew, German, Mexican, Thai, Native American, Congolese, and Nigerian, to mention a few. Everyone can access records of their past lives if they tune into Spirit, commune with their Guardian Angel, and journey into the Second Heaven where the *Book of Records* is kept.

During my sojourn in solitude, I was taken back to the times of Moses; the period man lived on another planet before destroying it, the times of Elijah, and when Jesus lived on Earth. I met with Saint Francis of Assisi, Pope John Paul II, Pythagoras, Shamus-i-Tabriz, Jalalul din Rumi, and several other Lords, Saints, and Guardians. Some of what I heard and saw is in this book. Some more are in my other books. Others stay in silence.

Inter-Planetary Council and Police

Just like the United Nations General Assembly is the international council overseeing the affairs of socio-political life on the physical part of this planet, the Solar System also has a council of representatives of each of the planets. This body, which is unknown to any of the leaders of Terra, except the Guardians, oversees the smooth running of affairs on all planets. The Council makes laws and has something like a police force, ensuring the safety, development, and progress of all inhabitants in the Solar System.

As an example, several times, our astrophysicists have predicted an imminent collision with meteors that could lead to cataclysmic destruction on Earth. But in the last moments, these unruly but deadly floating rocks would miss the Earth by the whiskers. The astronomers were not wrong in their calculations. These miraculous misses were the handiwork of the Lords of the Interplanetary Council coming to the aid of helpless man by deflecting these celestial objects off their course.

As usual, man would sleep on, further basking in his highly cherished ignorant ways, and the tabloids would denounce the astrophysicists as charlatans.

Man is not represented by anyone that wears a similar body to those reading or hearing this. However, a few of the Lords, who are more advanced than any of us, who also live on Earth but in a supra-physical body and environment, represent Terra on the Council. Man, as we know ourselves, is not on the Council because we are backward compared to the inhabitants of other planets in our Solar System.

For instance, we eat coarse food, work for money, fight and kill one another, and are generally ignorant of our Source, mission, our destination, and the realities of the Higher Worlds, which we call Heavens, which exist side by side our physical environment. For the same reason, our scientists cannot detect what they call 'intelligent life' on Venus, Mars, and Jupiter because they cannot find traces of oxygen and water.

This assumption is a display of utter ignorance. On Earth, there are many colonies or kingdoms in the water, even around us, which are completely invisible to us. To bring it further home sound is a physical thing, but the human ear is sensitive to only a specific range of sounds. Anything below or above that range is undetectable, and that means non-existent to the individual. The dog, however, hears a unique sound produced by the dog whistle, which is just a physical whistle made to alert only the dog while the human is unaware of the sound being generated. Consequently, it will be a display of arrant ignorance if we say the dog is only crazy to respond to 'nonexistent' sound just because man cannot hear the 'dog sound'.

Life on Other Planets

There is intelligent life on other planets. There are very advanced beings, higher than man on the evolutionary scale. They do not eat the kind of coarse food we eat because they do not use a body as coarse as ours. But they are still living in the physical environment, except that the vibration of their bodies, buildings, and other amenities exist on a higher scale than ours. However, they can make themselves visible to us; they can come down to our level, as it were.

In the nearest future, Earth scientists, under the guidance of the Lords, will develop highly advanced equipment for detecting sound and light at a higher frequency and velocity, and they will be able to 'download' them through specialized software to render them as recognizable images and sound to the human eye and ear. Then, it will be possible to watch life on other planets from the convenience of our homes or on our handsets, just as people on other planets watch us at present. And they have been watching for a very long time.

Close Encounters and the Ambassadors

Due to the evil, wicked, and ignorant nature of man, this planet is under the danger of being destroyed either by weapons made by man or collision with asteroids, meteors, meteorites, broken blocks from a dead planet blown to pieces by mankind (or man-un-kind) a long time ago. In addition, our evil or coarse aura affects other planets negatively. With these three elements put together; the Interplanetary Council has decided that life on this planet must be restructured. For thousands of years, some volunteers, very kind and highly spiritual Lords, from our neighboring planets, especially Venus, Mars, and Jupiter, have been coming around to influence life positively.

Some came as priests, philosophers, artists, musicians, scientists, while others came as exemplary kings, presidents, businessmen, teachers, architects, doctors, and farmers. They were born as children of men, but those who could see realize they were higher than ordinary men. In their rank include Jesus, Mohammed (*Sallalahu 'Allahi wa Sallam*), Shamus-i-Tabriz, Krishna, Rama, Buddha, Moses, Plato, Aristotle, Pythagoras, Socrates, Saint Francis of Assisi, Michael Jackson, Mary the Mother, Albert Einstein, several kings and queens of England and the European Emperors, and Shakespeare.

Most of them did not live perfect lives, but they did one or two things to promote love, wisdom, freedom, and the evolution of man from a selfish, self-destructive, limited being into an expansive, selfless Spirit-being.

The other mode they have used to influence life on Terra is a subtle manner of teaching our best minds in the dream state and during quiet moments. They send what we call inspiration and uplifting concepts and ideas. They perform what we call miracles either at religious gatherings or in our private lives.

A more direct mode of contact is physical and visible; through the use of spacecraft we call Unidentified Flying Objects (UFOs). They have been using these for ages, but man has always referred to these crafts either as 'moving stars' (seen by the three wise men when Jesus was born), 'pillar of cloud' (during the Jewish Exodus), 'Chariot of Fire' (Elijah), 'flying horses' (John in *Revelation*) and 'Unidentified Flying Objects' (ignorant, contemporary man).

Out of Time

Their mission has always been surreptitiously executed. They subtly infiltrated to warn, teach, and guide mankind. But man has not really obeyed and moved quickly on the path of progress. The forces of self-annihilation are quite formidable amongst the human race. As steps are being taken forward, so are some elements dragging man backward. Through destructive music, food, drugs, brainwashing, propaganda, pseudo-religious teachings and practices, black magic, worship of materiality, and the worship of human idols, a blanket of dark energy is thrown over the little Light that is struggling to shine.

Man has run out of time. The Soul of the planet, the Guardians of the human race, the Interplanetary Council, the Council of Saints, and the Lords of Justice have agreed that a more direct action be employed. The events leading to this Day of Justice and Direct Action are chronicled in this book. Events predating the recorded history of man are also chronicled in this book. How life will be during the reign of the coming 'Savior' of mankind — and the aftermath are also captured here.

We Are All Responsible

Under divine guidance or direct instruction from the Guardians, I have written prophetic letters to a cross-section of leaders of Terra. These include leaders of nations, continents, religions, women, and youth. Everyone has played a part in pushing man and the planet to the precarious precipice we have found ourselves. Everyone also has a role to play in salvaging the planet.

But man does not need visitors to know the right thing to do. You do not need the police before thinking right. This book contains specialized daily practices that can be done by people of all faiths and those without one, who are ready to transit from being a limited man to an expansive, happier, more loving HU-man.

Man must fulfill his destiny of being a God-directed, conscious, living Spirit, imbued with all the glorious attributes of the Source, otherwise called God. We shall all be happier when we do, so will the planet, our neighboring planets, the Solar System, and the Universe. There is so much goodness, loving-kindness, agelessness, ecstasy awaiting us in the new Earth and in the Heavens.

Science of Prophecy

Prophecy is a probability of the future. Whatever is seen and recorded at this minute can still be amended, if not eliminated. On one condition: Every individual involved in the foreseen future increases the quality of life they are living. By quality, I am not referring to an increase in material well-being but a significant increase in the loving thoughts, feelings, words, and actions being generated. This will, in turn, produce a better environment, more purposeful governance of human affairs, better religion, better science and technology, etc.

Many skeptics will doubt the possibility of a miraculous turn-around in the mindset of mankind within a few decades when the golden words of Krishna and Jesus have not been heeded for millennia. This is where individual karma or responsibility comes in. Everyone has their own separate account, even though our money is in the same bank, so to speak. If the bank were to be liquidated, every customer would be compensated based on their individual balance.

Day of Justice

For this reason, everyone is held accountable for all actions taken by him or her, be it while awake or asleep, be it in the material or mental worlds. When the Day of Justice and Direct Action comes, each will receive what they have earned. Those who are compatible with the upward mobility of Spirit shall be allowed to stay on Earth or proceed to one of the Heavens. Those who willingly and willfully disobey the directions of Spirit shall be removed and 'demoted', or banished to a more primitive, harsh planet which John called 'Lake of Sulphur and Fire'.

This book is part of a last-ditch effort sponsored by the Guardians of the human race to give every individual the opportunity of entering the Kingdom of Heaven while living on Earth or meriting citizenship of the new Earth coming soon. I hope you will read and listen to the words. But more importantly, you will take the keys that have been revealed here, apply them to create a more loving life for yourself. This will automatically make a slight but meaningful improvement to the future, fortune, and fate of Terra.

For a more comprehensive program on how to tap into the resources within you and to apply these to achieve a more rewarding life, please get a copy of my book, *Soul-Fullness*. Many people worldwide have used it to see their future, receive healing, discover their talents, get a better job, and even find a loving partner.

Holy Name, the Word, Rushing, Mighty Wind

Copious mention is made of 'Holy Name', and 'The Word'. These are the Sound or Voice of God put into words to make them easy to represent or identify. These words each carry powerful currents of the Holy Spirit. Every religion has them. There are JEE-SUS, YE-HU-VAH, ALLE-HU-JAH (Alleluia), ALLAH, ALLAH-HU, HU-MAN, RA-MA, RA, HU, OM, SHAN-TI, and many more. Personally, I have chanted, sung, or prayed with all these Words and others not stated here. The most striking for me is the HU, which is the rushing, mighty wind. In the Spirit, I have heard it coming from the Bosom of God like a roaring wind that cleanses all, transforming everything in its path. It goes, HUUUUUUUUUUUUUU endlessly, unbroken. The Apostles of Jesus had the privilege of hearing and becoming one with this Wind of God, the Word that was with the Source in the beginning.

I have also met several Muslims, followers of Krishna Consciousness, Buddhists, Christians, ECKists, followers of Native American religions, and African religions who have experienced this Word. What is common with all of them is the Light in their eyes, the Love in their hearts, the compassion in their aura, the confidence and humility in their attitude, their power to bring change and freedom everywhere they go and to all they meet.

Some people sing it, some pray with it; others listen to it, in their hearts, in the wind, in all uplifting songs and music, in the sounds of nature. They are uplifted by so doing.

There is no human being that has not chanted this Word. Every baby is born with it on its lips. Whenever a child (or an adult) is touched by an experience that strips them of all the veils of society, they hum a song or cry in a wailing tone that goes, 'Hu-Hu-Hu-Hu'. The rhythm is determined by the occasion and the feelings attached to it. In a nutshell, when you are happy or sad and you chant that Sound you are simply calling unto God either to give thanks or to surrender for help. God has designed it so. With this Word, everything came into existence. Your philosophical or theological disposition is inconsequential. Truth does not beg for belief.

Every other sacred Word contains the 'rushing, mighty wind' embedded in it. You can try it out if you have not. Before you sleep or while reading this, listen to all the sounds that you hear. Then, one after the other, eliminate all sounds produced by animals, humans, or machines. As if at the top, or back of your head, you will hear a sound like static, like waterfall, or like when water is boiling or steaming. Listen to it and concentrate on it. After a while, if you are ready, on top of this sound of boiling water, other definite sounds will be superimposed. It may be the sound of a flute, violin, running water, a loud church bell, aircraft engine, and cricket, or twittering of birds. Sometimes, either now or in the future, you will hear the 'rushing mighty wind'. You may be in church, in contemplation, in the dream, in the mosque, driving, in the shower, or chatting with friends. It will come when your heart or mind is focused on uplifting, loving thoughts and feelings.

Blessed are you, for you have been lifted into the Presence of God. Subsequently, changes will follow; changes that will lead you to deeper wisdom, more love and creativity, charity and forgiveness, courage and service to all life.

Pray It

An effective way to enter into the Bosom of God is to pray with this Sound. To do so, sit in a chair or lie in bed, close the eyes, focus on a holy person you know, or a person you love, or a place, an occasion that has brought deep joy and happiness to your heart, or just the space between the two eye-brows. Breathe in and out to relax the body and mind, then take a deep breath and sing the Word on the outward breath: "HUUUUUUUUUUUUU". Then, breathe in again and sing it when you breathe out; repeat the process for about ten minutes. After this, remain silent while you listen to the Sound, or the Voice of Spirit, or a Guardian

Angel. You may also see the spiritual Light. After about five minutes, just surrender your day, worries, and cares to Spirit.

You can do the same with the sacred Word 'Jesus'. Sing it in two syllables: 'Jeeeee-Suus'. Same applies to 'Aaaa-Laaaah' or 'Aaaa-Laa-Huuuuu' or 'Jeeee-Huu-Vaah' or 'Aaa-Le-Huuu-Yaah', etc. Stick to what works for you. But be regular with it. Pick a time in the morning and at bedtime to do it or when is most convenient for you. Make it daily.

If your heart is open to Love, by loving yourself and every creature of God unconditionally, you will experience the Wind and the Fire of the Holy Spirit. You will meet with the Lords. You will enter the Presence of God. You will become a more loving, wiser, and happier person. You will enter the Kingdom of God while still on Earth. This is the message brought to humanity by Jesus, Quetzalcoatl, Ju Chiao, Mohammed (*Sallalahu 'Allahi wa Sallam*), Orunmila, Zoroaster, Krishna, Pythagoras, Plato, Saint Francis of Assisi, Mother Teresa, the Dalai Lama, Gurumaa, George King, and Harold Klemp.

Not a Religion

This is not a new religion. The world has more than enough religion. What is lacking in the world is Spiritual Freedom. The offspring of that are wisdom, courage, love, kindness, happiness, and the creativity of Soul to turn what God has given to fabricate a pleasant environment, be it physical, emotional, or intellectual and spiritual, for self and others. The road to it is the Narrow Way lit by the Inner Light and directed by the Sound, the Roaring Wind of Heaven, the Voice of God.

I am here to strengthen your faith in yourself, your Source, your God-given power to be the best that has ever been created because it is pleasing unto the Source, the Lords, and yourself to be so, whether you have a religion or not. This is what the coming of the World Savior and visitors from other planets will enforce. But you do not have to wait. Take your future in your hands, right now!

As you read *The Book of Prophecies*, I am certain the power of Spirit's Love, Wisdom, Peace, and Freedom (salvation) will come alive in your heart, and happiness incomparable will burst forth like a massive waterfall in your life.

— *Tosin King James*

THE AUTHOR

James is a dramatist, screenplay writer, an experienced journalist, talk show host, and producer. He began writing when he was 12 and has had professional experiences in every genre of the literary arts. He distinguished himself in college as a playwright and administrator, going on to work in radio, television, advertising, banking, and publishing.

Privately, he has been a keen researcher, student, and teacher of practical spirituality.

He was born into the Pentecostal church by parents who were both Christians but had been born Moslems, converting after marriage. His father, James Snr, was a mystic versed in African, Islamic, and Christian traditions. Elizabeth Sarat, his mom, was an exemplary lover of Christ who had been blessed with conscious journeys into the Heavens a few times while alive.

Early in life, James was baptized by the Holy Spirit

during a Holy Ghost convention; he saw and was bathed by the Golden Fire and heard the silent Voice of God. This marked a turning point in his spiritual quest for The Word, which had begun while in the fourth grade.

He subsequently prayed, worshipped, and studied with several spiritual groups and bodies including Islam, Krishna Consciousness, Grail Movement, The Assemblies of God, the Catholic Church, The Apostolic Church, Deeper Life, Aetherius Society, and Eckankar.

He looks forward to being a cheerful servant of life, like the Saints, Guardian Angels, and Masters, who have taught him so much.

GLOSSARY

Ab initio: From the beginning; at the beginning.

Alchemy: Transformation from an ordinary to a higher, extraordinary state of consciousness; medieval concept of a change of base metals into gold.

Alfa: Priest, teacher in the Islamic Faith.

Alhaji: (Also, El-Hajj, Al-hag, Al-hage, etc.); a Muslim who has been to Mecca on holy pilgrimage (Hajj); used as title in West Africa to designate a devoted Muslim who has been to Mecca.

Alhamdu lillahi: Arabic for 'All praise be to God alone', or 'All the praises and thanks be to Allah'.

Allah: Aramaic word for God, the Creator, all powerful and all knowing; used by both Muslims and non-Muslims to mean God, especially by followers of the Abrahamic religions, including Islam.

Ancient One: Usually refers to God, the Creator, Source and Sustainer of all Life; the Spirit of God that man makes contact with.

Angel: See **Guardian Angel**.

Apeta: Yoruba word literally meaning, 'to call to damnation'; a metaphysical process by which someone is cursed via a spell cast upon the victim by a black magician; the victim, if without any spiritual protection, would die or run mad instantly.

Astral (body): The subtle, starry body, next to the physical body. It looks exactly like the physical body, but finer, younger, and more luminous. It is the body man uses when asleep and when dreaming.

Aura: A cloak of light made of invisible energies that surround the physical body of humans, animals, plants and rocks. It is composed of a mixture of thoughts, emotions, and physical energies utilized by the individual. It has been photographed by highly advanced cameras.

Avernus: A crater lake in Italy, regarded in myths and legends to be the entrance to hell; used by mystical writers to denote the Lower Astral regions that border the Earth, a place where Souls that were mean to others while on Earth would go at the death of the body.

Babalawo (Also Babalao in Latin America): Yoruba word literally meaning, 'father of the mysteries' to denote the priest of the Ifa Oracle. Traditionally, a Babalawo is a priest who is also versed in herbal medicine. He is a prophet and a very holy person. In modern usage, however, it may connote a black magician who casts evil spells on others for a fee.

Baptism of the Holy Spirit, or Holy Fire: the mystical version of water baptism, an immersion into or union of the individual with the Fire of Spirit, at the instance of a Celestial being or Power called the Holy Spirit. From reports, this mystical event comes with heightened awareness, wisdom, and other spiritual abilities.

Cartesian: Referring to ideas and theories propounded by French mathematician and philosopher, René Descartes (1596-1650 CE); most popular statement being "Cogito, ergo sum" meaning "I think; therefore I am".

Celestial Music: Heavenly Music, the Voice of Spirit heard as music or sound, usually uplifting and liberating.

Chi: Igbo language: the personal god, or Soul; Japanese: the vital life-force sustaining all things.

Creative Fiat: Creative command; creative decree; creative Word; the command uttered or issued by God to bring Creation or Life into existence.

Guardian Angel: A Spirit being assigned to guard and guide a living person, family, organization, country, or race.

Higher Power: Any source of power above and beyond the average human consciousness, with the ability to effect change or provide guidance, healing, and redemption; used in *Soul-Fullness* to refer to the pure Spirit.

Holy Spirit: An aspect of God that makes contact with mankind, to teach, guide, heal, and transform. It can be experienced as pure Light, Voice, Sound, and It can take a form, be it human or otherwise, to communicate intelligently with man, for the purpose of passing across a spiritual message.

Ifa: A system of divination of Yoruba origin. It has evolved over several centuries as a religion with the main focus on prophecy via intercessions made to Orunmilla, the prophet (or god) who introduced the system.

Imam: Leader of an Islamic community, mosque, or congregation, usually of the Sunni sect.

Jumaat: Islamic special congregational prayers, held after noon on Friday.

Karma, Law of: Of Hindi origin; action that determines the fate of a person, group, nation, or planet; whatever anyone sows, same shall they reap; action and reaction are opposite and equal — opposite in direction and equal in effect.

La ila illalahu: Arabic for 'there is no God but Allah', or 'no other power or god above God (the creator of all Life)'.

Malaika: Arabic (and many other languages) for Angel; Malaak is sometimes used as the male version.

Mana: A word of power, present in several religions across the world; power to make things happen, or manifest.

Marijuana: A psychoactive drug extracted from the cannabis plant, used for medical or recreational purposes. Abused, it has the power to alter the state of consciousness beyond the control of the user, therefore exposing them to possible psychic dangers.

Master: A spiritual guide with the ability to teach, guide, heal, and uplift the student, both awake and asleep.

Medium: Someone or something that serves as an intermediary between a living person and a dead person.

Medulla Oblongata: Continuation of the spinal cord into the brain stem; control centers for the heart and lungs.

Metaphysics: An esoteric branch of philosophy, engaged in the exploration of concepts and theories of life and existence; practical demonstration of the power of mind over matter, with regards to miracles and magical phenomena.

Morse Code: A system of communicating, using a series of on-off tones, lights, clicks, or sound, with a set meaning that can be understood by someone in the know.

Moslem: An adherent, or follower, of the Islamic faith.

Mosque: A place of worship for followers of Islam

Naira: Nigerian currency

NUTASA: Nigeria Universities Theatre Arts Students Association; comprising of students of theatre, dramatic, and performing arts in all the Universities in Nigeria.

Nutasaite: A member of NUTASA.

Phallus: The penis; a symbol or representation of an erect penis, especially in reference to male potency.

Pharaoh: Ancient Egyptian title for king or head of the kingdom.

Prophecy: A prediction of a future event or situation, either by pronouncement, vision, dreams, day-dreams, intuition, or other forms of knowingness.

Psychic: A person exhibiting knowledge or powers beyond the five senses with reference to the control of people, places, and situations to suit the wielder of such abilities; in reference to paranormal abilities, activities, and energy.

Purgatory: In Catholic doctrine, a way-station between Earth and Heaven where sinners are purged of their sins, after which they may be allowed to enter Heaven.

Quran: The holy book of Islam, consisting of messages from Allah delivered by Archangel Gabriel, or Jibra'il, to the Prophet Mohammed, *Sallalahu Alaihi wa Sallam*.

Salalahu Allahi wa Sallam: Arabic phrase meaning 'May Allah honor him and grant him peace'. It is commonly used after saying the name Mohammed when referring to the founding Prophet of Islam.

Salvation: The doctrine of Christian origin that man is a sinner and must be redeemed through belief and faith in Jesus, the Christ, otherwise the individual would not enter into Heaven. Islam has similar beliefs without anchoring it on Jesus, but on a total faith and submission to Allah.

Satan: Originally meaning 'one who opposes, obstructs, or causes harm'; in Judeo-Christian and Islamic traditions, it refers to a personification of evil as opposed to Light, Love, and God.

Soul: A Unit of Spirit; the true identity of all living things; indestructible, genderless consciousness that uses mind, emotions, and the physical body to express Itself; see **Spirit**.

Soul-Fullness: A 21-Day D-I-Y program developed by Tosin King James to help the practitioner become aware of their identity as Soul; the process and essence of seeing and operating as Soul.

Source, The: The Creator, God, Higher Power.

Spirit: The vital element that keeps nature alive; a disembodied being; that which distinguishes a living being from a dead body; the power of God that keeps everything alive; also an Angel.

Spirit Beings: Souls who exist in extraterrestrial environments, with supernormal abilities; humans who have left the Earth and are operating in a high spiritual realm.

Spirit-Son: (Coined by Tosin King James); refers to the personification of God in the role of a redeemer of mankind from a limited, selfish being, to a limitless, selfless individual, who becomes a conscious co-worker with Spirit or God. The Spirit-Son relates with each Soul, using a form recognizable to the individual; usually assuming a male form, He has the ability to teach, guide, and heal every being either awake, asleep, on Earth, or in any of the Heavens. From the dawn of time, He has incarnated in the body, or personality of a chosen individual, with the main purpose of giving the message of Love and Freedom to all living Souls. He has been encountered by people in different locations and times on Earth. Many religions have recognized His presence in or around their leader.

Spiritual Ear: An inner faculty in every human being by which esoteric sounds — different from physical sounds — can be heard and understood. This faculty is employed to hear the Voice of God, Angels, and other Spirit Beings.

Spiritual Eye: An inner faculty in every living being with which spiritual Light, sights, and visions — beyond the normal physical range — can be perceived. In the human body, it is situated behind the spot between the two eyebrows, corresponding to the pineal gland, which is a physical channel through which the Soul seeing abilities are expressed in the body. The pineal gland itself is not the Spiritual Eye but a channel for the latter.

Spirit Realm: A place beyond the physical world inhabited by living beings. It is sometimes called Heaven in religious literature. It is accessible to every human who can operate as a conscious Soul or Spirit even while alive in a physical body. There are several of such realms.

Sufi: A follower of (or belonging to) a deeply mystical order in Islam. Generally, the body of beliefs and practices are referred to as **Sufism**, though there are many variants.

Sufism: See **Sufi**

Third Ear: Same as **Spiritual Ear**.

Third Eye: Same as **Spiritual Eye**.

Tisra Til: Sufi term for **Third Eye**

Voodoo: A religious and mystical practice combining an element of Catholic and African rituals, dependent on spiritism, necromancy, possession by discarnate entities, and magic. It is widely practiced in West Africa, the Caribbean, and parts of the USA.

Yoruba: A race of people with ancestral headquarters in South Western Nigeria. They can be found in several West African and American countries. They speak a distinct language also called Yoruba. There are over 50 million native speakers of the language, with more than 20 dialects. In South-Eastern USA, the Caribbean, and South America it is also a religion, originally practiced by people of Yoruba origin taken as slaves from West Africa.

www.ingramcontent.com/pod-product-compliance
Lightning Source LLC
Chambersburg PA
CBHW011232160426
43209CB00009B/1561